Peace in the Brokenness

What others are saying about Gina Holm and

Peace in the Brokenness...

"I am excited to recommend my ministry friend, Gina Holm's book, Peace in the Brokenness. Gina is a gifted teacher, speaker, writer, and leader of women, helping them discover who they really are in Christ Jesus. I would also highly recommend her for any teaching or speaking opportunities. Her story is one of God's grace and His power to heal. Women will not only relate to but also find healing and encouragement in their journey with God."

—**Les Morrison**, MA, LPC
Re: Connect Counseling and Consulting Services

"Gina has a fervor for encouraging women find their wholeness in Christ. Her writings prove a steadfast commitment to God's Word; her words communicate and speak relevant approaches to spiritual well-being and maturity."

—**Elaine Stone**, Pastor's wife and writer

"My wife and I have known Gina and her husband for the better part of a decade. Gina's book, Peace in the Brokenness, is full of real battle-tested truth from the life and heart of a sincere Christ follower. Gina has learned how to trust God in challenging times and difficult realities. You will discover truth in her book, to be sure. But because it is being applied to Gina's personal experience, you will also find life. Sit back, grab a cup of your favorite drink, and prepare to also drink in hope."

—**Tom Bourke** , Detroit City Director , Navigators Ministry

"Gina's heart is not only for God, but also for the women around her to grow in their love and obedience of Him. I am one of the many women who has benefitted from her passion, investment, and unswerving commitment to "do the hard things" in Scripture. Her godly wisdom has been forged through many difficult seasons, and her testimony of God's faithfulness throughout them resonate true. She is one of the most down-to-earth, fun, godly women I have the joy of knowing. To spend time with her is to have a Titus 2 moment. I am so thrilled for God to bless even more women through her book, *Peace in the Brokenness*!"

—**Liz Cobb**, Gina's mentee and friend

Peace
in the
Brokenness

*Peace is Not the Absence of Brokenness
in Our Lives, but His Presence in the Midst of It*

Gina Holm

NEW YORK

NASHVILLE   MELBOURNE

Peace in the Brokenness
Peace is Not the Absence of Brokenness in Our Lives, but His Presence in the Midst of It

Published in New York, New York, by Morgan James Publishing. Morgan James and The Entrepreneurial Publisher are trademarks of Morgan James, LLC. www.MorganJamesPublishing.com

The Morgan James Speakers Group can bring authors to your live event. For more information or to book an event visit The Morgan James Speakers Group at www.TheMorganJamesSpeakersGroup.com.

Shelfie

A **free** eBook edition is available with the purchase of this print book.

CLEARLY PRINT YOUR NAME ABOVE IN UPPER CASE

Instructions to claim your free eBook edition:
1. Download the Shelfie app for Android or iOS
2. Write your name in **UPPER CASE** above
3. Use the Shelfie app to submit a photo
4. Download your eBook to any device

ISBN 978-1-68350-006-3 paperback
ISBN 978-1-68350-008-7 eBook
ISBN 978-1-68350-007-0 hardcover
Library of Congress Control Number:
2016904956

Front Cover Photo Provided By:
Kim Schuler

Cover Design by:
Rachel Lopez
www.r2cdesign.com

Interior Design by:
Bonnie Bushman
The Whole Caboodle Graphic Design

In an effort to support local communities, raise awareness and funds, Morgan James Publishing donates a percentage of all book sales for the life of each book to Habitat for Humanity Peninsula and Greater Williamsburg.

Get involved today! Visit
www.MorganJamesBuilds.com

Table of Contents

Acknowledgements

If you ever meet someone who tells you that writing a book is a walk in the park, or simply putting words on paper, don't believe him! Yes, the author might be the one who writes the words, but everyone close to you will feel like they have written at least a portion of the book with you. And in a way, they have. It is not without their support and sacrifice that this kind of dream becomes a reality. They put up with editing deadlines and the sharing of their personal stories. They feed you when you forget to eat, and they keep your cup of coffee full, literally and figuratively. They pray you through your stuck moments and cheer you on. None of them ask or want any of the credit for it. Trust me, they don't. But I must give thanks! Where do I even begin?

To Almighty God! My Maker and my Savior. The One who never leaves me nor lets go of me. He is my everything, and I am nothing without Him. May the words in this book serve only to bring glory to His name and peace to our hearts, and to help move His kingdom forward.

To my family: my husband Lindell and our three kids, Caleb, Jacob, and Elli. What a journey we have walked! I love you each with a love I simply can't find words to describe. Thank you for loving me when I am hard to love. Thank you for your endless support and encouragement. Thank you for being patient with me when my brokenness rears its ugly face. I thank God for the gift of mercy He has given me in each of you. May we never forget Whose we are and who we are.

To two of my dear wiser-than-me friends: Kelly and Beth. Thank you for your faithfulness to the kingdom of God first and showing me what it means to "Go, and be about the Fathers business." Thank you for your endless prayers for me and my family. Thank you for your friendship and loving me enough to ask the really difficult questions while gently holding my hand along the journey. This book is now part of your legacy and my attempt to pour into others a small amount of what you both have poured into me during one of my driest seasons yet...living water.

To my editor: Kelly Battles. Her job was so much more than adding a million commas, periods, and rearranging words to provide a better flow to my message. She pushed me and kept me real with her faithful "I need you to expand on this" or "dig a little deeper and insert a personal story" in all the right places after a revision. She started out as my editor, but she has become a faithful prayer warrior and friend.

And last but not least, to Morgan James and the entire publishing team. You took a chance on me as a new author by inviting me into the Morgan James family. What a privilege and honor it has been. A million times over, thank you!

Introduction

Do you ever wonder if true and lasting peace can be found in the midst of the chaos all around you? We all long for peace, the kind of peace that elicits a beautiful picture of a sunset above still waters with birds in perfect flight. But it doesn't take long for that picture to be interrupted by the brokenness all around us. Sickness comes our way; careers come to an end; dreams are shattered; relationships crumble; marriages fall apart; and children rebel. Human trafficking is at an all time high. There is brokenness - all around us! Before we know it, we start allowing for that brokenness to define us and the ever-so-dangerous game of comparison begins.

We live in a world in which we are told that we can just trade in whatever is broken in our lives for what feels good. What we don't often hear is that the reason we feel

> We live in a world in which we are told that we can just trade in whatever is broken in our lives for what feels good. What we don't often hear is that the reason we feel broken is because we are.

broken is because we are. We may not all be broken in the same way or to the same depth, but broken is broken. Until we understand the *why* of that brokenness, peace will only be temporary. There is no hope in that! And where hope is absent, that true and lasting peace we all long for cannot be found. Whatever your brokenness looks like and wherever your brokenness has led you, be encouraged. Look up, my friend—there is hope! Peace can be found! Peace is not the absence of brokenness and chaos that's all around us; peace is God's presence in the midst of it all. How do I know? Because that has been the case throughout my very own life.

The truth is, I had no idea that what started out as journals to help me process a season in my life would bring old and new brokenness to the surface, resulting in a book. A book that was born out of a wiser-than-me friend's question: "What does peace look like here, Gina?" The book you are holding in your hands is a mix of my story and the tools God showed me as I dug into His Word, the Bible, to find the answer to her question. I honestly did not see this book coming, but here it is!

The first couple chapters lay the foundation for the journey. Chapter One will help you get a better understanding of what peace really is and why we long for the beautiful sunset and still waters with birds in perfect flight. Chapter Two explains the *why* of the brokenness which interrupts that glorious picture of peace we all long for. My prayer is that you will be encouraged to see that there is *beauty* in the brokenness. From Chapter Three on, we navigate through choosing peace as we learn to use specific tools for the journey ahead.

It is my prayer that you will be encouraged and empowered with the stories and the tools found in this book. Each chapter concludes with questions for personal reflection and application, or group interaction.

Will you join me in this journey? Great! Let's get started and turn to Chapter One. I want you to know that I pray for you often...even from afar.

Because He is God,

Gina

Psalm 46:10

Chapter One

What is Peace?

*E*arly in May 2003, I took our son, Jacob, to the doctor. He was four months old, and things just didn't seem right. Although he was born at a healthy weight of 9 lb 9 oz, he had not been eating much and seemed to be in constant discomfort.

After the doctor did his examination, he said, "Mrs. Holm your son has a condition known as Hirschsprung's. It is a condition of the large intestine, and it is very serious. I believe your son is in great danger. If the toxic levels reach a certain point, there may be nothing we can do for him. The ER at Children's Hospital is waiting for you right—"

I interrupted him and said, "Can you please write down what you just said to me? You see, I am going to call my husband in a few minutes, and I am not sure I will be able to communicate to him what you just said. Because all I have heard is that my son is in great danger, and the ER is waiting for us."

So he did. He quickly wrote it down for me and then went on to say, "I know this is not easy news to hear. I am so sorry, but I need to you to realize the urgency. I need to know if you can drive him the twenty-five minutes to the hospital, or if you need me to call for an ambulance."

It was one of those moments when auto pilot kicks in, and I just move forward. I called my husband and went. He started heading to Children's Hospital, but he was two hours away. As I pulled into the ER, they were indeed waiting for us. My heart was beating 100 miles per hour as I ran alongside a gurney answering a million questions. They moved so fast, getting him ready for a series of tests and emergency surgery.

After all the testing was done, the surgeon walked in to give me the results, explain the condition, the procedures needed, and the risks involved. As I was holding ever so tightly to my baby, the doctor said, "Mrs. Holm, I am going to need you to hand us your baby."

With the most respect I could find, I calmly said, "I am sorry doctor, but I don't know who you are. I don't know where you went to school or how vast your experience is with these cases." (I later found out he was among the leading surgeons in the nation!) "I haven't had the chance to interview you or check your references. And you are asking me just to trust you and hand you my baby without a guarantee I will get him back alive." I can't find the words to explain the anxiety my heart was feeling in that moment.

The doctor's tone then changed, and with great compassion in his voice he said, "Mom, I have never been on the other side of this conversation. I can't even imagine what that would feel like. However, I promise you we will take good care of him. We need your baby, and we need him now."

So, with trembling arms and weak knees, I handed the medical team my Jacob. But you see, the only reason I could do that was because in that moment, I had to make a decision: while I was handing my baby to the medical staff, I was placing my baby boy in the arms of Jesus. But I didn't like it. And I didn't understand it. However, in that moment of surrender, tears ran down my face while I watched them walk away with my sweet boy. As I waited for my husband to arrive, God gently whispered in my heart, "Gina, Be still, and know that I am God" (Psalm 46:10). And while God's promise was not that it would all work out the way I wanted, I was able to start working my way back to peace.

While that moment happened over thirteen years ago, I can still remember it as if it was yesterday. And as I sit at my local coffee shop, typing these words for you right now, tears run down my face once again. I can still smell the crisp, clean smell of the waiting room as a janitor was cleaning the floor near me. I can see the face of that sweet nurse bringing me a warm cup of coffee. She offered a gentle smile and said, "I will be right here if you need anything." But what I remember most and will never forget was the stillness my heart felt, as second by second I surrendered my fears and anxiety back to God saying, "He is Yours, Lord! But please, Lord!"

The anxiety, the fear, and the *brokenness* I was experiencing did not change the fact that He remained God. Because of that and that alone, I could be still. I could be at peace because peace is not the absence of brokenness in our lives, but it is God's presence in the midst of it. Thank You, Lord!

That was the beginning of a crazy, long, four month journey. Jacob endured four major surgeries, and each time we didn't know if he would make it through. There were endless emergency room runs where my prayer was simply, "Lord Jesus! *Help!* Please give me all green lights. Please let me get there on time. Please don't take my baby Home! I will be still and know that You are God." And as I walked through the ER doors each time, I found myself singing, "Hold me Jesus, because I am shaking like a leaf. You have been King of my Glory; won't you be my Prince of Peace?" And that He was, my Prince of Peace through it all.

What is peace? "Peace" is a small word that is often used and gets a lot of attention. We all long for peace within ourselves as well as the world at large. We are all familiar with the brokenness our heart and soul feel when we hear about children dying from hunger, and the horrors and nightmares of human trafficking. And we wonder if world peace can ever be achieved in the midst of all the brokenness and pain.

At one point or another we have all wondered if there is more to life than what we are currently doing. Whether we have nothing left to give or whether we have all our boxes checked, our hearts still long for peace. Often, words get thrown in as a cliché answer: "I hope you find peace in this situation." But cliché or not, those words resonate in our hearts, and we hold on to hope. We memorize Bible verses about peace, and these verses help us find our way back to peace. But

> We memorize Bible verses about peace, and these verses help us find our way back to peace. But then we wonder what to do with the brokenness that remains.

then we wonder what to do with the brokenness that remains. Yes, we all long for peace, and most are even willing to go on the quest to find it. But it's not long before we lose heart as we hear of more brokenness in the world around us, and we get to feel the aching of that brokenness when it hits close to home. We go back to wondering if peace can ever really be found.

One of those wondering moments for me came on September 11, 2001. Most of us can still remember that sinking feeling as we watched the horrifying scenes of the Twin Towers, the Pentagon, and that field in Pennsylvania as planes crashed into them. I remember standing there in unbelief. My heart broke and then sunk as I thought of all the people who had just lost their lives, people who kissed their families as they walked out the door and went about their day, but would never come back home. I thought of the first responders who ran in towards danger in the hope of rescuing even one life, but in the process, they gave up their own lives. I could only imagine the horror as their families watched everything unfold right before their eyes on their TV's. As I held our month old baby, Caleb, near my heart, I ached for the kids who would not be picked up by their parents from school or daycare that day or any day after. Then it all started to sink in. My heart became heavy and anxious. There were too many unknowns.

Being a Marine Corps wife when September 11th happened, I knew that life would change quickly. It's not that it took me by surprise. I mean, I did marry my man in uniform and knew there was more than just how incredibly handsome he looked in that uniform the day I said, "I do." But there is a difference between knowing the day would come and standing in our living room holding our baby knowing that day was now here. From that moment on, the only thing that could be expected was the unexpected, and even that could change at a moment's notice. During deployments filled with long nights full of prayer, I would eagerly wait for his next phone call.

I remember how my heart felt as if it skipped a beat when I finally got to hear his voice again on the phone. Sometimes the conversations were difficult, and sometimes we laughed the whole time talking about the simple things of life. Whichever way the conversation went, when the time came for the call to end, there was always a short, heartfelt silence. I would find a way to smile and just say, "You come back home to me, okay? I love you," hoping that it wasn't the last time I got to say it. Every time, God whispered to my heart, "Be still, and know that I am God" (Psalm 46:10). That verse has been my life verse for years, and while the verse didn't promise that everything would work out the way I wanted it to work out, it always brought my focus back to God, and I started my way back to peace once again.

I mentioned that while we memorize Bible verses and the verses help us find our way back to peace, we often wonder what to do with the *brokenness that remains*. Let me explain what I mean. Lindell was on deployment, and the house was finally quiet. I was looking for something to watch on TV when the news flash reported a helicopter down, and Marines killed. But there was no other information in the news report. As it usually was when those situations happened, all communication went down, and I held tight to "no news is good news" as I prayed my heart out. It was the longest night of my life as I wondered if there would be a knock at my door.

When the phone finally rang and I heard the sound of his voice, I simply wept. I couldn't talk. He just kept saying, "I'm here, Baby Doll. I'm here." I had never been happier or more thankful to hear his voice before. Yet, as thankful as I was, my heart continued to break. While I was thankful and at peace that my husband was still alive, I wrestled with *the brokenness that remained*. I knew that there were four families whose doors had been knocked on. I knew there were four families who had been notified. I didn't know them, but it didn't matter. I didn't have to know the families to know a fraction of the pain they were living in. Yes, I wrestled with the brokenness that remained.

I wrestled with the guilt of the wife that would not get to say one more time, "You come home to me, okay? I love you." I wrestled with the brokenness of children not having their daddy at the dinner table that next Thanksgiving and every holiday thereafter. Yes, all of that brokenness was real, and it would remain. But that didn't change the fact that God remained God. It also didn't mean that there could not be a knock at my door next time. I still had to choose to "Be still, and know that He is God." It is only when I have surrendered to His promises that I find peace even when brokenness remains. Circumstances don't change the fact that He remains God, and like the good Shepherd, He holds me close to His heart.

Now, I don't believe you have to be married to the military to understand what I just shared. No matter our background or career choices, we all know that it is just a matter of time before the next bad thing happens and difficult times will come our way.

Yes, brokenness still remains. There is no promise that even now there won't be a knock at my door with some horrendous news. In fact, just last week I got a phone call with news that my dear friend was diagnosed with a rare cancerous tumor in her heart and is getting chemo treatments while fighting for her life. There is no promise that the chemo will help, the only promise we have is that He will remain the God who never leaves us, and He will never let go of us. Because of that, I can be still and know that He is God. I find peace in that.

I don't believe all the brokenness takes us by surprise, but when we are standing in the middle of it, it sure can shake us to the very core of who we are and leave us longing for peace, wondering if peace can be found again.

We often hear or read of many people and organizations around the world that devote a lot of their time and resources in their quest for peace. They share great ideas in the hope of coming up with plans for how to be at peace. There is this idea that if the world could just get along, peace could be had, and it could be enjoyed by all. There is this idea that in order to have peace, *all* brokenness must come to an end.

Some people would define peace as knowing that everything is going to be "ok" even though they find themselves in the midst of brokenness. Others define peace as the absence of that brokenness and the conflict it brings. Others define it as life simply being "just so."

In the process of researching what people think about peace and how they resolve brokenness and conflict, I discovered that the United Nations sets one day aside every year called the International Day of Peace. All nations represented get together for the purpose of hearing from others as well as sharing their own thoughts and plans to promote and create peace around the world. They have held this day and remain committed to its purpose since 1981 when it was first established by the UN General Assembly.

Shortly after reading about the United Nations, I found myself reading about the Nobel Peace Prize. According to *The Oxford Dictionary of Twentieth Century World History*, every year since 1901 this prize has been awarded to the person or organization that "shall have done the most or the best work for fraternity between nations, for the abolition or reduction of standing armies and for the holding and promotion of peace congresses."

Lastly I came across a well-written article that promoted a similar sentiment as the two previous organizations except it was geared towards personal peace. The writer shared his passion for peace and shared his well thought out plan and intentions to achieve it. He had wonderful ideas of getting people together of all different backgrounds and cultures to identify ways they could learn to get along. However, in his recommendations he strongly communicated that if we were going to strive for personal peace and learn to get along with each other and other cultures, all religion would need to be set aside and out of the conversations as spiritual matters were controversial and would only cause disruption to any possibilities of finding peace.

Please know that I am not criticizing any of these organizations or persons. We can see they are willing to get the conversations started at the personal level and the world at large. I commend them for their efforts and desires to make our world a better and more peaceful place by taking the time to find ways in which peace can be found in the midst of the brokenness that we read and hear about daily in the news.

The author of the article on finding personal peace specifically requests to leave any kind of spirituality and religion out of the process of finding peace and mending the brokenness. The idea to leave all spiritual matters out of the process for finding peace is, in my humble opinion, one that makes little sense. Yet while it makes little sense, it's an idea that I am familiar with and can understand.

I can understand the author's desire to leave spiritual matters out, because while I was growing up, I had an idea of who God was. But I tried to leave God out of my quest in finding the peace my soul was longing for. However, it makes little sense to leave God and spiritual matters out because our spirits, our very souls, are longing for peace. And God as the Creator of our souls is the only one who can provide the permanent kind of peace I believe the UN is trying to achieve, the Nobel Peace Prize is wanting to award, and the author of that article, like all of us, is trying to find.

I grew up in a wonderful family that could have been cast in a movie called *My Big Fat Mexican Wedding*. I have many wonderful memories of being in a family who, although we have our share of struggles, cared for and loved each other deeply. We regularly shared family time at my grandparents' house on Sundays. One of my favorite childhood memories is swimming in my grandparents' pool and hearing my grandma say "Vaya con Dios" (go with God) at the end of our visit as we would leave her house to go home.

We didn't go to church regularly, but I knew there was a God and that His name was Jesus. I knew He died on the cross for my sins and that He would be coming back some day. The problem was that while I knew all these things about Him, I didn't *know* Him. I didn't understand that His rules were not simply suggestions for living, but the foundation for finding peace. Instead I tried to find peace by conforming to whatever my friends and others thought I should be. I figured that if I could just measure up to others' expectations of who I was supposed to be, I would be enough, and they would never leave me.

As a result, try as I might (and believe me I tried), true and lasting peace was nowhere to be found. I searched high and low, but unfortunately as the song says, I went "looking for love in all the wrong places." When I say "all the wrong places" I mean anywhere God's rules were not necessarily a strong foundation for living. They weren't ignored; they just weren't always the priority. The "wrong places" became comfortable places for me because, truth be told, I was angry with God, and I spent a good portion of my life running away from Him.

I was angry with God because some of my first memories of Him where that of a distant God, a God who didn't care much for the cry of a heart wanting to be rescued from the nightmares of losing my Father. My dad had a heart condition and had already survived two heart attacks, his first one being at the age of 39. My dad always told me that I was the apple of his eyes and what kept his heart beating. So when he didn't survive his third heart attack at the age of 49, it was nearly impossible to understand how a loving God could take a nine year old girl's dad just weeks after he had promised that he would never leave. My dad had promised me that as long as I was around, he would always be there. In my distorted view of God, I blamed God when anything bad happened. I mean, if He was so powerful, why couldn't He keep my dad alive? If He was so powerful, why couldn't He stop bad things from happening? All of it just felt cruel of Him, a supposedly loving God.

As a result, I concluded that I didn't want much to do with that kind of God; I thought of Him as more of a "genie in a bottle" instead of a Holy and merciful God. I decided when He could have access to my life and what areas of my life He was allowed to enter, like on the occasional Sunday morning when it worked with *my* plans to go to church with my family or with my friends. Yet, I did whatever I wanted the rest of the time, in between the occasional Sunday visits. I called on Him only when I wanted Him to rescue me from the hurt or the consequences of my actions. I made deals with Him. You know, the "Ok God, if you are real…" or "I am going to give You one more chance to rescue me from the mess I've created for myself…" But the rescue didn't come the way I wanted it. So instead of asking Him to reveal Himself to me as who He was—God—like a pouting toddler, I said, "See! I knew You didn't care." And I put Him back in the genie bottle and walked away. If I didn't have a wish or something to be rescued from, He was confined to the bottle, and I would not think much about Him again until the next rescue was needed.

Well, the next rescue came on Sunday, May 3, 1992. I had been out with some friends the night before. The unwise choices we made that night were an attempt to run from the brokenness I felt, but I woke up feeling broken once again. However, broken and all, that Sunday was the day my heart cried out to be rescued from the emptiness and the continual brokenness resulting from my poor choices. I had a friend who regularly invited me to church, and that morning I said, "Yes, why not? Nothing else is working, and I am tired of this pit that I have created for myself."

I will never—not ever—forget what my heart felt when I first heard the words, "Because God has said, 'Never will I leave you; never will I forsake you'" (Hebrews 13:5). It was one of those moments when it felt as if I was the only one in the church, and the pastor was speaking directly to me. All of the sudden, I realized that the One I had been angry with and running from was the only One who could make and keep that promise. Not my dad. Not a boyfriend. Not a friend. Not anyone else.

I couldn't help but get down on my knees at the end of the church service and weep. While I wept, I felt the gentle hand of a sweet older gentleman on my shoulder as he sat on the pew, quietly praying for me. When I could finally look up, he asked, "Honey, are you ready to give your life to Jesus?" To which I responded, "Yes! I have never been more ready to do anything else in my entire life." I prayed the shortest and simplest prayer, "Lord Jesus, I surrender. I am a sinner in desperate need of a Savior. Please take my life, and the brokenness of my heart, and make it whole." And with that short and simple prayer, for the first time in my life I was at complete peace.

Please don't misunderstand me. My circumstances didn't change. In some respects, it was the beginning of them becoming more difficult. But it didn't matter; for the first time in my life I experienced the peace that surpasses all understanding as He welcomed me into His presence. And ever since that day, He has been answering my prayer for the brokenness of my life and has made my heart whole again. What a Savior!

We all long for peace in our personal lives and the world at large. But our great ideas and plans don't work when we make it a point to leave God and all spiritual matters out of the conversation. Great plans are, well, great. But even the greatest and well-thought-out plans can't stand when attempted to be carried out on a crumbling foundation absent from God through His Son, Jesus Christ. With that in mind, let's take a look at peace and how it can be found in the brokenness of our world and in our own personal lives.

While people may define peace differently, there is a common picture that describes what we long for. Peace is often thought of as a beautiful, serene picture, capturing the still waters with the sunset in the background, and a couple of peaceful birds in graceful flight. Peace is captured by a painting that communicates harmony, agreement, and order. Peace is often described as the absence of conflict, brokenness, and hurt.

Don't be discouraged here. The description of the beautiful picture with peaceful still waters and sunsets with birds flying is indeed a picture of peace, although for me, I would need to change the scenery a little bit to include an ocean with a hammock or chair and my feet in the sand, or preferably in the ocean's warm water, holding a cup of coffee! Whatever your ideal picture of peace is, it is important to understand that these glimpses of that peace on this broken side of heaven will remain just that, mere glimpses of peace.

Don't feel bad for longing that the glimpses become permanent. God has not forgotten about you when your glimpses of peace have faded. There is a reason and explanation that our hearts long for that picture of peace. There is also a reason and explanation that until Jesus returns or takes us home, our pictures of peace will remain mere glimpses. We will talk more about that in the next chapter. Until then, be encouraged! Peace can be found in the midst of the brokenness of our lives. It just looks a little different from the glorious picture we find ourselves painting and longing for in our hearts.

> God has not forgotten about you when your glimpses of peace have faded.

With that in mind, let's now take a look at what the scriptures have to say about peace. In the Old Testament, the primary Hebrew word for peace is "shalom." It translates to completeness, soundness, and welfare. Shalom is often found in the context of a covenant relationship with Almighty God. "'Though the mountains be shaken and the hills be removed, yet my unfailing love for you will not be shaken nor my covenant of peace be removed,' says the LORD, who has compassion on you" (Isaiah 54:10). We also find that there is a direct connection of peace to Jesus and the promise of His coming for the restoration of His kingdom. "For to us a child is born, to us a son is given, and the government will be on his shoulders. And he will be called Wonderful Counselor, Mighty God, Everlasting Father, Prince of Peace" (Isaiah 9:6).

In the New Testament, the primary Greek word for peace is "eiréné," translating to quietness, rest, and peace of mind. This peace comes as a result of our relationship with God being restored through salvation in Jesus.

While it is important to understand the Hebrew and Greek translations, simply put, peace is a gift that can only be found in Jesus Christ: the baby in a manger who we celebrate at Christmas and the Lamb of God who was crucified on the cross for our sins, victoriously raised from the dead by the Father on Easter. He is a Father who loves us so much that He would stop at nothing to provide a way to restore us back to Himself. He longs to give us that beautiful and glorious picture of peace for which we all long. It is in this Jesus—God in the flesh, Emmanuel, God with us—that peace is found. He, and He alone, is peace.

It has been the prayer and longing of my heart that you will find peace in the brokenness as you take your next step in your journey with Him, be it for salvation or in your sanctification process.

"I pray that out of His glorious riches He may strengthen you with power through His Spirit in your inner being, so that Christ may dwell in your hearts through faith. And I pray that you, being rooted and established in love, may have power, together with all the Lord's holy people, to grasp how wide and long and high and deep is the love of Christ, and to know this love that surpasses knowledge—that you may be filled to the measure of all the fullness of God" (Ephesians 3:16-19).

I will never forget when I finally understood that, regardless of the brokenness and messiness of my life, God loved me! He just loved me. There was nothing that I could possibly do to earn or lose His love. He loved me because I am His. Prior to embracing that truth, while there were moments of happiness and fun, they were often dependent on circumstances. I think happiness is wonderful! I love being happy, who doesn't? However, happiness is often dependent on something good happening, and therefore, it also is just temporary. It wasn't until I embraced the truth of Ephesians 3 that I didn't just find happiness, I was able to find true joy. Joy is dependent on nothing other than our relationship with Jesus. As we surrender our lives to Him, circumstances may stay the same, but we find true and lasting peace.

On one wonderful morning, I had the honor to lead a friend to the cross of Jesus for salvation. After she prayed and gave her life over to Him, she looked at me. With tears in her eyes, she asked, "Gina, what is this? The problems are still there, but what is this peace that I am drowning in?" I smiled and said, "That, my sister, is the Holy Spirit of God taking residence in you." Galatians 5:22 tells us that peace is an attribute of the fruit of the Spirit. While we still may wrestle with the brokenness that remains, the word of God tells us that, "the peace of God, which surpasses all understanding, will guard your hearts and your minds in Christ Jesus" (Philippians 4:7). You see, true peace, the peace that we read all throughout scripture, has very little to do with our circumstances and our surroundings, and everything to do with a merciful and readily available God. He is the only One that remains the same yesterday, today, and tomorrow. That is good news! That is peace!

The good news doesn't end there. The good news continues as He wants us all to have that peace. It all starts with that simple and short prayer I shared with you when I gave my life to Christ. If you don't know Jesus, stop right now. Ask Him to search your heart, and with that simple and short prayer, you too can meet the Prince of Peace!

If you prayed that prayer for the first time, it is my privilege to welcome you as my sister in Christ to God's family. You have no idea the party that is going on in Heaven because of you right now! I want to encourage you to find a local, Bible teaching church and get connected. We all need a church family to help us grow. God designed it that way. Now, keep in mind that there is no perfect body of believers. If there were, there would be no need for the cross. It is, however, of utmost importance that you find a church that has sound, biblical doctrine.

If you have prayed the first part of that prayer before, and have been walking with Jesus for a while but needed to pray the "Please take the brokenness of my life and make it whole" part of the prayer, be encouraged sister! You are in good company. We must take heart in knowing that "He who began a good work in you will bring it to completion at the day of Jesus Christ" (Philippians 1:6).

As I dug in deeper and researched the topic of peace and brokenness, I conducted surveys of women of all ages, both with faith backgrounds and nonbelievers. I discovered that we women can be creative and come up with great ideas to fix our brokenness. Some dive into exercise and health improvements, while others work to climb the career ladder. Some look for their soul mates, while others lose sleep trying to figure out how to fulfill every need in their children's lives, hoping to spare them from brokenness. Each one of those things can be a worthy activity. However, I also discovered that it is only in knowing Christ and surrendering my all to Him, that I stop pursuing my own idea of peace and how things should be. In part, the problem is that in this rushed culture of immediate gratification, we want Him to make everything the way *we* think it should be. We want all the wrong to be made right. We want all the brokenness to be made whole. And we want it *right now*! If we get really honest, sometimes we want to get even with those who have hurt us. We think that maybe justice will bring us peace. We want whoever played a part in the pain to feel some of it. I know, I know. I get it! But, we must not confuse revenge with justice. While doing so, we might feel justified with our hurts validated, but that is not peace. That is just getting even, and the feeling won't last. It will just be a matter of time before something else comes our way.

Time and time again we find in Scripture a reference to peace pointing to Christ, the purpose of His coming, and His character. The gospel of Christ is often referred to as the gospel of Peace. It makes perfect sense since the only reason for His coming was to make it possible for us to have peace with the Father. He came "to give light to those who sit in darkness and in the shadow of death, to guide our feet into the way of peace" (Luke 1:79). Scripture also tells us of our inner peace being directly connected to our seeking "first His kingdom and His righteousness" (Matthew 6:33). If I am seeking Him, His kingdom, and His righteousness, I don't need to fear or worry about what is to come. I can be still, knowing that He takes care of the rest. I can have peace.

I am fully aware that this world has a way of reminding us that brokenness remains. We don't have to look very far to see that there is turmoil all around us. Sickness comes our way, careers come to an end, dreams are shattered, relationships crumble, marriages fall apart, and children rebel. The world at large is in chaos. If we are not careful, we take our focus off His righteousness and once again get distracted by the circumstances around us. We so quickly lose sight that it is only that which is built for His kingdom that will last. We make the tragic mistake of letting our minds become a playground for Satan, his lies, and the condemnation they bring. Yet Scripture tells us clearly that, "there is now

> We so quickly lose sight that it is only that which is built for His kingdom that will last.

no condemnation for those who are in Christ Jesus" (Romans 8:1). In order for us to have a solid foundation for peace to endure the brokenness of life, we must understand His righteousness first, that fullness of God I have been praying for you from Ephesians 3.

His righteousness is for us to be in a right relationship with God. We know that can only happen through Jesus' work on the cross. We have spent a good portion of this chapter connecting peace to His righteousness. So if peace is directly connected to His righteousness, it would only make sense that His word is what defines the lines and sets the boundaries for peace. I don't know about you, but being the free-spirited girl that I am, I had to learn to embrace the idea that boundaries are good. When I first started walking with Jesus, I thought boundaries kept me from being free. My idea of boundaries was that they were restrictive. Unfortunately, it wasn't until after some scars and a few bruises (that disobedience to the Word of God can bring), that I learned it is only within the boundaries of His Word that freedom can be found. I then learned to appreciate and embrace those boundaries.

Boundaries let us know when we are within His will, or when we have stepped out on our own, focusing on our circumstances instead of His righteousness and His peace. It is when we are outside of the boundaries that we soon lose perspective, and with that, we lose our peace. Those beautiful boundaries let us know where we are standing and what is needed to start working our way back to peace when we have wandered off.

So if peace is about the righteousness of God, what does His righteousness look like? While there are many passages of Scripture that teach us about His righteousness, I think this passage in Philippians 4:8-9 is a good place to start:

> Whatever is true, whatever is honorable, whatever is just, whatever is pure, whatever is lovely, whatever is commendable, if there is any excellence, if there is anything worthy of praise, think about these things. What you have learned and received and heard and seen in me—practice these things, and the God of peace will be with you.

The challenge in that verse is the *"practice these things"* part. It requires creating enough space in our lives to be still, that we may *"think about these things."* It calls for us to be intentional, disciplined, and obedient. It is only out of obedience that the blessing flows. The blessing? The reward? His peace! Then we are "filled with the fruit of righteousness... to the glory and praise of God" (Philippians 1:11). It is in that place of peace with Him and there alone, that while there may still be a few monsters under our bed, they no longer keep us awake at night and paralyze us with fear.

Ah, fear! When our kids were little, we watched our fair share of *Veggie Tales*. I am not sure if you are familiar with that cartoon, but there was a song in one of their episodes that I still sing quietly when fear comes my way: "God is bigger than the Boogey Man. He's bigger than Godzilla and the monsters on TV [or under our beds!]. Oh, God is bigger than the Boogey Man, and He's watching over you and me." I know it's just a silly song, but it is a silly song full of truth. It is a silly song reminding us that God is bigger than...you fill in the blank. And with that simple and silly song, along with the truth found in His word, our peace has its strong foundation!

Yes, we will continue to struggle with not letting go of our peace this side of Heaven. I know I do. It is only when our foundation is without cracks that we find our way back to peace, even if we wrestle with the circumstances of life. It was just a few weeks ago that I found myself in the struggle of circumstances around me, and my peace was a little shaken after a conversation took me to places I don't ever care to remember. You know what I mean. We all have those places that while healing has happened, raw memories and deep emotions can easily be found. I felt so defeated and crawled under the covers and started to make that tragic mistake of letting Satan use my head as his playground.

I am thankful that it wasn't too terribly long before I realized I was outside the boundaries of peace. I had allowed my mind to wander. I had to make the conscious decision in that moment to start fighting my way back. However, I would be a fool to think that I could fight the enemy of my heart, mind, and soul on my own. I cried out to the only One who can fight those battles for me, "Lord Jesus! Take my hand. Please walk me back." I started saying Scripture out loud and was reminded that, "We destroy arguments and every lofty opinion raised against the knowledge of God, and take every thought captive to obey Christ" (2 Corinthians 10:5). What that simply means is that we have to measure everything by what God's word says. If it doesn't line up with scripture, it doesn't matter how real the emotions may feel or how convincing the lies may sound; they remain just that, lies.

It was through saying out loud who God says I am that I was reminded, while those things had been true of me in the past, I no longer was them nor was I defined by them. I am God's creation, and that gives me my worth and my identity, as I was created in His image. I am a daughter of Almighty God, and He calls me to walk in His truth. Yes, the list of things that used to define me is long but, "By the grace of God, I am what I am, and his grace to me was not without effect" (1 Corinthians 5:10). The effect of His grace in my life has conquered my sin and the identity that once held me captive. My identity is now found in nothing other than in me being His beloved. He loves me because I am His. I don't know about you, but that brings me peace. That causes me to stop striving to please others and start thriving as I make my way to being still before my God. That brings me back to peace.

I am not saying there aren't times in which we shouldn't explore our wounds so that healing and closure can be had. What I am saying is that we should not make the mistake of letting our enemy keep us defeated. Yes, we need to get the appropriate help. I know I had to. But when the wound finally turns into a scar, after Jesus sews every stitch, we should not make the mistake of allowing our enemy to keep tearing it open only for us to drown in the wound again. Yes, the pain is real, and our scars have their purpose. Their purpose is not to pick on them. They are simply there to remind us of our deliverance and the healing that has taken place. Yes, we each have our wounds, but, "By his wounds we are healed" (Isaiah 53:5). When we embrace that truth, we soon realize that, while we never forget how much it hurt when the wound happened, we can stand victorious, and with an overwhelmed heart say, "Thanks be to God, who gives us the victory through our Lord Jesus Christ" (1 Corinthians 15:57).

Earlier I mentioned that peace will require being intentional, disciplined, and obedient. We must be intentional to have moments, maybe even seasons, of true stillness, not just a fifteen minute rushed reading shot of Jesus. Those are good and needed, but won't sustain us while in battle. I have found that it takes time for my mind to truly unwind from every distraction around me. For this girl, everything quickly turns into squirrels, if you know what I mean. It takes time for me to really open up my heart and say, "Search me, O God, and know my heart; test me and know my anxious thoughts. Point out anything in me that offends you, and lead me along the path of everlasting life." (Psalm 139:23-24). I hate to say this, but truth is truth, and the truth is that I have yet to pray that verse and have Him say to me, "It's all good, Gina! There is nothing to work on here. Carry on." Why? Because He has not yet returned, and I am still on this broken side of eternity. Yes, I try to live out my salvation, but I remain a sinner saved only by the grace of God. Does that mean that there are boulders of sin in my heart every time? Not really. But I guarantee that there is always at least a grain of sand to be removed. And man, have I seen a small grain of sand do some damage to a wood floor…just like a grain of sin in my heart.

I have this great passion for God's word for a reason. Being the broken woman I am, and the fact that He seems to have given me an extra dose of emotion, if I am not careful, my emotions (while good and often well intended) will run wild. His word, while it can cause conviction to my heart, must be the final authority in my life. By doing so, I can stay as close as I can to His righteousness, peace and the rest it brings to my sometimes weary soul. So as corny as it may sound, I don't know how to breathe without His word, and I don't recommend you should either. In times of foolishness, I tried to be at peace, but didn't stay close to His word because I thought I just might have a better plan. Those times have only caused wreckage, and I have nearly been taken out.

When my focus has not been on His Word but on the circumstances around me, I have been known to slam doors and throw dishes into the sink (not very peaceful of me). While some could say that in some of the cases, my hurt and anger could be justified and my behavior understood, God still calls me to peace in the midst of brokenness, not in its absence. He calls me to get *my* heart right and not worry about what others do with theirs. He calls me to turn from *my* sin and not wonder what others will do with theirs. Yes, this is difficult, especially when the wounds and pain run deep, which is all the more reason we need to get to the foot of the cross and do what it takes to be healed. Make no mistake; God will take care of their hearts.

> "Never be wise in your own sight. Repay no one evil for evil, but give thought to do what is honorable in the sight of all. If possible, so far as it depends on you, live peaceably with all. Beloved, never avenge yourselves, but leave it to the wrath of God, for it is written, 'Vengeance is mine, I will repay, says the Lord'" (Romans 12:16-19).

Remember, getting even is not peace, and it's never worth it. Holding on to the pain and anger will only hold *us* prisoners. Letting go does not mean that those who wronged us will get away with it. Letting go, forgiving, and trusting God to take care of the situation simply sets our heart free so peace can be found. Besides, while I also have been known to go all "Mexican" on people, there is no amount of vengeance I can give that will compare to the wrath of God. After not getting it right many times, I have learned that I don't want to get caught in the middle of God dealing with anybody else's sin but my own. I have plenty of my own sin to deal with. I don't need to pick up anybody else's. We can only work on our own brokenness. We are only responsible for our own sin and what we do with it.

Yes, that beautiful picture of peace toward the beginning of this chapter is wonderful and definitely a glimpse of what peace is. But for now, and until Jesus returns to turn this upside down world right side up and makes the brokenness whole again, we must hold tight to the words spoken by Jesus in John 16:33, "I have said these things to you, that in me you may have peace. In the world you will have tribulation. But take heart; I have overcome the world." Sweet friend, we must remember that the accurate picture of peace is not the absence of brokenness and the conflict it brings, but His presence in the midst of it. We must take heart in His promises!

I know that in the busyness of life, it can be difficult to make time. Please know that I don't get to just sit at His feet all day long. I am just as human as everyone else. I have responsibilities just like anyone else. I end up with crazy days in which I am tired even before I wake up. But for the wellbeing of my soul and the safety of the heart of those around me, I've had to become intentional and make time to have more than my "fifteen minute shot of Jesus" at least once a week. It usually means that I have to say "no" to something else, and it's usually not one of my responsibilities. But I promise, spending time with Jesus is worth every second of the sacrifice to keep my focus on His righteousness. For our hearts to "Be still, and know that [He is] God" (Psalm 46:10), we must be disciplined to store up His word in our heart so that we might know the boundaries of His righteousness and not sin against Him (Psalm 119:11).

Now, I must keep it real here; the hard part about this is that we must put what we read in His Word into practice and live it out. It is only in applying His Word to our lives that we will bring about transformation. The million dollar question I find myself asking on a regular basis is, "What does active obedience look like in my life today?" Notice I didn't say *perfect* obedience. I said *active* obedience. It means that we are actively and intentionally trying to live out our faith as best as we can, so that His blessing of peace may reign in our hearts.

I remember a wiser-than-me (older) friend once said that we must make it a point to regularly examine our hearts and to keep a short account with our God if we want to remain at peace. His word tells us that we cannot have peace without His righteousness. Sin must be called what it is, sin, and it must be confessed so that His "righteousness and peace kiss each other" (Psalm 85:10). My wiser-than-me friend then asked me a simple, yet profound, question, a question that has changed my life. Truly, it did. She asked, "What does peace look like here, Gina?" It was out of that simple, yet profound question that this book was born. It was out of that question that the next exercise I want to share with you came about. Shortly after my friend asked me that important question, I went home and grabbed one of my giant post-it papers and circled the word peace in the middle of it, then worked my way around the circle.

Yes, peace can be found in the brokenness! Yes, it will require work, but it will be worth it. He believed that bringing us peace was something worth dying for. We must believe and do our part knowing that His peace is worth fighting for. I say it again, take heart!

This exercise was born out of that simple yet profound question my wiser-than-me friend asked, "What does peace look like here, Gina?" Because the result has been so profound in my life, it is a tool I use regularly to keep my heart in check and as close to peace as possible for longer stretches.

Now it's your turn. Set some time aside, grab your bible and work through the exercise.

Exercise

1. Name the circles in your life where you would like to experience peace. Be as specific as possible. Example: Finances, career, family, ministry, marriage, parenting, friendships.

2. Look up specific Bible verses that speak to each "circle" in your life. Based on the verses you found, ask yourself, "What does peace look like here?" Follow the example on the graphic below.

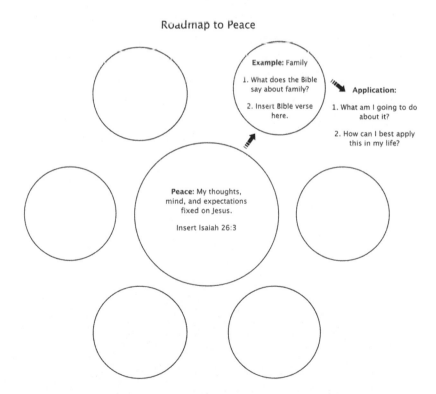

Roadmap to Peace

Example: Family

1. What does the Bible say about family?

2. Insert Bible verse here.

Application:

1. What am I going to do about it?

2. How can I best apply this in my life?

Peace: My thoughts, mind, and expectations fixed on Jesus.

Insert Isaiah 26:3

The verse I work through when doing this exercise is found in Isaiah 26:3

> *"You will keep in perfect peace all who trust in you,*
> *all whose thoughts are fixed on You."*
> *Isaiah 26:3 NLT*

As I identify the areas in my life in which I am not trusting Jesus, I can start working my way back to peace by fixing my thoughts and expectations on Him instead of my circumstances. When I do that, peace enter.

I know it wasn't easy because it took time and effort, but now that you have completed your exercise, you have your boundary map to stay at peace and to find your way back to peace when you most assuredly, like me, will wander off. Keep it in a place where you can see it or get to it easily. I can't tell you the difference it makes to have quick access to this exercise when old or new brokenness comes your way. Even when it is a familiar brokenness, when something new comes with it, we are once again vulnerable.

Chapter Two

In the Brokenness

I was working on a project and looking for a specific picture on my phone's camera roll when I came across a picture that was taken by my daughter, Elli. Even though she is nine years old, I continue to call her my "baby girlfriend." She took this particular picture while playing on my phone, waiting for me to be done with physical therapy. I was in pain, and the picture showed it. Let's just say it's not one of the most flattering pictures of me. I almost deleted it, but then something caught my attention, and I stopped when I realized that I was actually thankful for what it captured.

In 2004, while patiently waiting at a red light, I was used as the stopping point for a drunk driver's out-of-control vehicle. The accident caused permanent damage to my neck which continues to get progressively worse. My doctors are helping me adjust and find solutions in this next season of pain management, so I began physical therapy again recently.

The picture I discovered was taken when I was at the end of my session and what felt like the end of my rope. I wanted to delete it, but not because it wasn't the most flattering picture. I wanted to delete it because when I looked at it, there is no denying that there was pain involved. When I look at this picture, it shows that there is no way around the reality that I will be dealing with the pain for the rest of my life. If the doctor's prognosis is right, the pain will continue to get progressively worse. Since the pain can already be debilitating at times, I didn't want to look at the picture. Instead, I wanted to run from the brokenness it represented.

If I am not careful, in the midst of the pain, I can sometimes find myself dangerously close to a pity party. And sometimes I belly flop right into the pit. When the pain is high, frustration kicks in, especially since my pain comes as a result of the consequences of someone else's actions.

But here is the thing about that picture that caught my attention. Without knowing, my baby girlfriend captured a moment of my pleading with God. My neck was wrapped with ice, and my eyes were closed. My pleading with God was not for Him to take the pain away, even though I know He is more than able. My pleading with God in that moment was to find peace with the prognosis, trusting He will provide whatever is needed, every step of the way. I was pleading with Him to help me be joyful (not happy) in the midst of the pain. My plea can be found in 1 Thessalonians 5:16-18, "Be joyful always. Pray without ceasing; in everything give thanks; for this is God's will for you in Christ Jesus."

I usually pray the verse backwards: "Lord, I don't understand. I don't like it. It hurts. I know You could fix it. But this is where Your will finds me right now. I will, therefore, not lose heart and will pray without ceasing that my joy will be found in You alone. I choose You. I choose to praise You in this moment. I am thankful that it wasn't worse. I am thankful for great doctors helping manage the pain. I choose joy knowing my children didn't even get a scratch. I choose to pray for that man. I pray that you would bring healing to whatever brokenness and pain *he* may have been running away from that day as he chose to drink too much and get in his car. Wherever they are, Lord, please bring healing to his soul and peace to him and his family."

If I am not careful, I forget how many spiritual DUI's I have been forgiven. If I am not careful, I get distracted by the pain and forget to thank God for His grace and mercy. It is only when I choose joy and am thankful for His faithfulness that I am able to find my way back to being still. Knowing that He is God, I am able to find my way back to *peace in the midst of the brokenness.*

Even though I was looking for a different picture, I believe I found this picture for a reason. It wasn't the one I wanted to see, but it was the one I needed. Oh the ever-so-humbling reminder that while joy and peace may look different in each one of us and in the different seasons of life, peace and joy should always be reflective of the One who gives them. No my friends, I don't always do it well; I don't always choose what is right. What am I thankful for today? Why am I joyful? I'm thankful for a better day, for His mercy and faithfulness that are ever so new every morning, and for a new opportunity to live out His message one more day.

Part One: The Why of Broken

Broken: made into pieces from a whole.
Busted Collapsed Cracked Crippled Crumbled Crushed Damaged Fractured Injured Shattered Smashed

Those are some of the words that come to mind when I think of something being physically broken. I can relate to some of those words because I've had my share of physical brokenness; my body has failed me more times than I care to mention.

My most recent series of physical brokenness included three major surgeries in a two year period. It felt as if I was not fully recovered from one surgery when the next one would come. It was a difficult season, taking its toll on our family for sure. As a matter of fact, my daughter was getting ready to go celebrate one of her BFF's birthdays with a sleepover at her house. All of the sudden she turned to me and very matter-of-factly said, "You know Mom, it is nice to have a sleepover without you being in the hospital for your surgeries."

Her innocent remark made me realize how difficult that was on all of us. Those same words at the beginning of this chapter are how I feel in the on-going physical brokenness of my neck and back. But we all know that our *physical* brokenness is not the only thing we experience. We also experience emotional and spiritual brokenness.

When I asked others what comes to mind when they hear the word "broken," they shared these words: problems, discord, unsettled, pain, a mess, fixing.

Some people define "broken" as something that used to be whole and perfect. It might sound simple, but it makes sense. I believe we would all agree that in order for something to be broken, it needs to start by being whole. It is from wholeness that pieces are shattered. You and I were created in the image of God; therefore, since the image of God is what gave us our wholeness, it only makes sense that Jesus is the only one who can make us whole again. He is the only one who beautifully displays the righteousness and mercy of the Father. "He is before all things, and in Him all things hold together" (Colossians 1:17). And that, my friends, is the only source of peace that can last, even when the brokenness remains.

Broken is a feeling that, if we are honest, we have all felt at one time or another. Although, we may not feel brokenness in the same way or to the same depth as someone else does. It can sometimes be difficult to identify the feeling as brokenness, because we often make the mistake of thinking that if our circumstances were different, we would not have ended up here, feeling so hurt, feeling so *broken*.

We may not identify our hurt as brokenness every time. However, when and *if* our hurt is finally identified, there is often a resistance to calling it *brokenness*. Why? Because being broken is often associated with something negative. We may not always have a solution for our brokenness, and we may want to delete it, much like I wanted to delete that picture of me at physical therapy, because there was nothing I could do about the pain. So we find ourselves wanting to quickly move from that negative emotion and hurt into a different place, a place where emotion won't leave us feeling so defeated and empty, feeling so *broken*. We allow ourselves to be distracted by the busyness of life. We can even justify our busyness with good things like running around from activity to activity for our kids, or by over-committing ourselves to helping in our children's classrooms, or by serving at church and in the community.

Whatever our *good things* are, they are not necessarily the problem. We should all do good things. However, when we do good things simply to fill up our schedules and feel accomplished, well, we are running from our brokenness and moving toward denial. And the crazy cycle begins again.

It makes perfect sense that we would want to move away from brokenness. Don't beat yourself up for it. Feeling broken doesn't feel very good. It certainly does not go along with the "We have the *right* to be happy!" mentality that at one time or another we have all declared. Our first thought is much like my wanting to delete the picture my baby girlfriend took at the end of physical therapy that afternoon. The reality of my physical pain and brokenness was staring at me right in the face, and there was nothing I could do to change it. It was difficult and uncomfortable to look at the picture at first. However, as uncomfortable as the brokenness may feel, understanding that there is a reason behind it will help us to better embrace it. We don't move forward when we avoid the brokenness or remain stuck, wishing that our circumstances would simply change. Thinking that if our circumstances could just be different, the circumstances would free us to move into the peace we all long for, the peace we are desperately seeking.

Brokenness has much to do with the condition of our hearts. Over the course of my life, I have personally experienced what we often refer to as a broken heart. I am sure you have also. It's that aching our heart feels when we receive news of a loved one passing away or when a relationship has come to an end.

When we hear the term "broken heart," our minds picture an image of a red heart with a zigzagged line splitting it in half. Well, wouldn't you know that there is an actual physical condition, legitimizing those times when we have experienced the physical pain of a broken heart? Until I started my research on this topic of brokenness, I did not know that there is an actual medical condition known as Broken Heart Syndrome. On its website, the Mayo Clinic defines this condition as "a temporary heart condition that's often brought on by stressful situations...In broken heart syndrome, there's a temporary disruption of your heart's normal pumping function... The symptoms of Broken Heart Syndrome are treatable, and the condition usually reverses." Much like the condition of our *spiritual* brokenness, the *physical* brokenness can only be reversed when we seek the treatment of the physician who specializes in "Broken Heart Syndrome." In the case of our *spiritual* brokenness, we must go to the Great Physician, Jesus, for our treatment and healing.

It is amazing (yet not surprising to me) that the medical profession would be able to diagnose the *physical* condition of a broken heart, which also captures so well the brokenness of our *spiritual* condition.

Much like the physical condition of Broken Heart Syndrome, the spiritual condition itself is not fatal unless it's not treated. According to Mayo Clinic, the damage of an ongoing broken heart can lead to death. So how does this connect to the spiritual condition of our brokenness? I believe that question can be best answered if we take a closer look at what the Bible has to say about us being created in the wholeness of the image of God; we were meant to live in the perfect world for which we all long.

Let me officially invite you to buckle up as we take a crash course and tour through the first few chapters in the book of Genesis. It will give us a front row seat to the human condition and help us understand this broken heart condition as well as our spiritual brokenness better.

In Genesis 1:2-25, we read that God spoke the world into existence: "In the beginning, God created the heavens and the earth. The earth was without form and void, and darkness was over the face of the deep. And the Spirit of God was hovering over the face of the waters" (Genesis 1:1-2). It was His spoken word that commanded light into being. The air, land, and sea were given their shape, and all the vegetation, plants, and living creatures were created and made by God. His creation of the world was not simply a transformation, but an actual beginning. And He said that it was all good (Genesis 1:25). Yet, even though His creation of the world was good, it wasn't until He created human beings in His image to live in this good and perfect world that God said that it was "very" good (Genesis 1:31).

What does that mean to be created in the image of God? It is important to understand that being created in the image of God is not of physical likeness, but of spiritual likeness. It was from the ground that

> *We get our identity and worth from our creator. Nothing else has the authority to define us.*

God gave Adam a physical body, and, for us women, it was from Adam's rib that we were formed. But we get our identity and worth only from our Creator. Let me speak this truth again: *We get our identity and worth from our creator.* Nothing else has the authority to define us.

It wasn't until God's breath entered us that we became a living soul (Genesis 2:7). Our soul is what sets us apart from the rest of creation. Our soul is made up of our mind, our will, and our emotions. We were created to reflect the fruit of His Spirit, which is "love, joy, peace, patience, kindness, goodness, faithfulness, gentleness, and self-control" (Galatians 5:22-23).

That is why it wasn't until after He created us that creation was completed, and then He said that it was very good. We were created to be in relationship with our Creator and walk with Him in the cool of day for eternity. The reason we long for that perfect setting of peace and companionship is because *that* is what we were created for. I often imagine what it would be like to walk with God along a beautiful beach when the sun is setting, and the waves are crashing. Birds are in graceful flight, and the wind is blowing on my face. And yes, I would be holding a fresh cup of coffee in my favorite big red mug (the one that broke a couple of months ago).

So, if we were created in His image and for a perfect world, why is there all of this brokenness? How do we reconcile a Holy and perfect Creator with all the brokenness in this world? I have wrestled with these questions myself. The answer is as simple as it is complicated. The answer to that question is found in Genesis 3, a chapter entitled "The Fall of Humanity." This is where our brokenness originated. It is the chapter in which, much like today, we see how we can be quickly tempted and deceived into worshipping the creation instead of the Creator.

Prior to this chapter of Genesis 3, the world and our image were perfect. Now remember, the image we are talking about is not a physical one. When Adam saw Eve, all he said was, "WOW!" There was no mention of her physical features. He was wowed by the reflection of God's image in her.

Back to Genesis 3. Sin entered the world when Adam and Eve ate the fruit of the forbidden tree. Wait a minute! Does that mean that there was sin in the tree that God created? No, not at all! In its simplest form, sin is *choosing something other than God.* There was no sin or anything special about that fruit. The sin referred to here is when Adam and Eve didn't trust God and ignored His instructions to not eat the fruit of the tree. As a result of their disobedience, Adam and Eve were no longer able to enjoy the beauty, creativity, and companionship of a Holy God and the world He created.

I know. It is easy to want to blame Adam and Eve for the brokenness. However, I submit to you that if it had not been them, it would have been any one of us. As a matter of fact, if we are honest, from time to time we can find ourselves doing the same thing: worshipping the creation instead of the Creator. It tells us so in Romans, "They traded the truth about God for a lie. So they worshipped and served the things God created instead of the Creator himself, who is worthy of eternal praise!" (Romans 1:25 NLT). Yes, we have all done that. I know I have.

Although the truth is that only God can fill the God-shaped hole in my heart, I believed the lie that I had a better plan, and I put my expectations and hopes in the creation that I could see and touch instead of trusting in my God. I put my hope in God's wonderful and precious creation instead of the Creator. I believed my wonderful husband could meet all my needs, or my precious children could make up for lost things.

Listen, when I have done that, I did not find peace. Frustration, anxiety, and disappointment are all I gain. I do have a wonderful husband and precious children whom God has used many times as a way to bring joy, healing, and restoration to my brokenness. But as wonderful and precious as they are, and try as they may, they will always fall short. Why? Because as wonderful and precious as they are, they are not God. They remain part of the creation, but they are not my Creator. As wonderful and as precious as they are, they are also broken beings.

A dear and wiser (older) friend of mine gently said to me once, "Gina, your children don't define you, and you don't define your children." There is a lot of wisdom in that nugget of truth. I encourage you to think about what your default is in your choosing creation over the Creator. It can be anything. It doesn't have to be a person. It can be your career, your ministry, your home, your Facebook friends and status, or how many followers you have in whatever social media outlet you choose. Anything that is not *God* is part of His *creation*. Sweet friends, we have to get honest with ourselves. No, it doesn't sound good or feel good to look our brokenness in the eye when we choose pride over humility. Often we believe we just might have a better plan than God. But until we embrace our brokenness, we will continue to choose whatever fruit the temptation represents. But I am getting ahead of myself here. Let's get back to Genesis 3.

In Genesis 3, Satan is first seen and identified as our greatest enemy in the long and ongoing battle between good and evil. We see the fall of humanity through Adam and Eve. The brokenness of sin entered the world, and life became overshadowed by it as our relationship with God was broken. That, my friends, is why we feel the brokenness today, because we are currently living in a Genesis 3 world.

Oh, but there is hope! We have hope that even though the brokenness of sin can still find its way into our lives, the story doesn't end there. We can have hope knowing that there is healing available to our brokenness right here, right now, today. His name is Jesus. And, oh how we need Him. Why? Peace without Him will always be temporary. I know that if there was a way we could just write a check and pay for peace, we would. As a matter of fact, I am sure that we do try to buy it. We may not think of it as buying peace per se, but we buy "that thing" we are sure will make us feel better, like that perfect pair of shoes I loved and thought were the best purchase for a quick pick-me-up on a cloudy day...until they broke as I walked in to meet with a publisher about this very book!

But "that thing" is different for everyone. Shoes may not be yours, but if you stop to think about it, you will figure it out. Every one of us would buy peace if we had the chance. Yet Jesus is the only One who can write the check for our brokenness. He wrote it with His life. Unlike my awesome pair of now broken shoes, Jesus brings permanent peace, regardless of the brokenness.

God also knows what a broken heart feels like. It is shortly after the fall of humanity in Genesis 3 that we see the heart of the Father, our Creator, breaking. We see His mercy and His compassion when, just like a parent, He seeks His children, even though He already knows they have done wrong. The story of redemption begins when He confronts Adam and Eve's sin. For the first time, we see the Father willingly sacrifice the first drop of blood of His creatures, creatures He lovingly created. You see, God sacrificed the animals he loved for the benefit of a human in rebellion. By doing so, He provided Adam and Eve with clothing and cover their shame. All the while, God pointed to the ultimate need for salvation in Jesus' death, God's one and only Son (John 3:16), on the cross and His extraordinary resurrection from the grave. What a Creator! What a Father! What a God!

Yes, the consequences of sin caused fear, brokenness, and shame to enter the world. And even though to this day we are the ones who have sinned against our creator, God remains the One who continually seeks to be in a relationship with us while we try to run away and hide in our shame. In *Unwrapping the Greatest Gift*, author Ann Voskamp reminds us that in our brokenness, "When we've fallen and when we're lost, God comes with one question. Not the question, 'Why did you do that?' Not the question, 'What did you do wrong?' The very first God-question of the Old Testament, of the whole Bible, is a love-question howling out of God's heart: 'Where are you?'" And today, He continues to ask the same question. He is a Father who loves us so much that He can't stand the thought of living without us, not because we deserve Him, but because we are *His creation*. Make no mistake, while we see the ugliness and brokenness of sin all around us, He remains faithful, constantly involved in the world He created, concerned with our human identity and our restoration. We just need to adjust our view and take a look through the lens of the story of God's redemption found in the Gospel of Jesus, the Gospel of peace.

Our *spiritual* brokenness is much like the *physical* Broken Heart Syndrome. It is brought on by stressful situations caused by our sin when, like Adam and Eve, we choose whatever the apple represents in our lives. The disruption is temporary because of Jesus' death and resurrection, which provides new life for Adam, Eve, and all mankind. For you and for me! The symptoms are treatable because we have the Holy Spirit available as our great counselor and healer. And we have the living word of God, the Bible, to help us find our way back when we have lost our way. And, here is the best part: the day is coming when the condition of our spiritual brokenness along with every other brokenness will be reversed! At His glorious return and the restoration of His kingdom, each one of us will be made whole and unbroken for eternity. He is coming back, sweet friend! He promised so in John 14:1-3, "Let not your hearts be troubled. Believe in God; believe also in me. In my Father's house are many rooms. If it were not so, would I have told you that I go to prepare a place for you? And if I go and prepare a place for you, I will come again and will take you to myself, that where I am you may be also."

However, as in the case of Broken Heart Syndrome, if sin and its brokenness are not treated, we will experience a spiritual death. The reality that we will spend eternity either in relationship with God or eternally separated from Him should give us a sense of urgency to embrace our brokenness and true identity in His image through the glorious work of Jesus Christ on the cross. And while eternity should propel us to be in relationship with Jesus our Savior, that relationship must start while we are still here on earth, by the way we chose to live our lives, and by embracing our brokenness, seeking His kingdom first, trusting Him to take care of the rest.

Sweet friend, I understand that we may not all be broken in the same ways. We may not all be broken to the same depth. But make no mistake about it—the reason we feel broken is because *we are*. Scripture tells us we are (Romans 3:23). But there is hope! Oh, there is great hope! The hope we have, the remedy to our brokenness and finding the peace we long for, is found in Jesus. There is no other way (Romans 3:24-26).

So, now that we understand the "why" of our brokenness, what's next? Interestingly enough, the antonyms of *broken* include the following words: perfect, whole, connected, continuous, fixed, flowing, satisfied, uplifted, complete.

I don't know about you, but I do have a favorite antonym: whole. Truth is, I really love every one of these words. They are all words that communicate the redemptive work of Jesus to save us from the brokenness. However, since it is from wholeness that brokenness comes, whole is the one that resonates most with me in brokenness.

I believe that we all long for these words in our lives. The good news? They can be had, my

> We embrace the brokenness and its beauty through the surrendering of our pride.

friends! However, it requires that we embrace the brokenness and its beauty through the surrendering of our pride. We foolishly hold on to pride, thinking that we just might have a better idea, that there might be another way to find peace. Oh, sweet friend, trust me, when I was foolish enough to believe my idea was better, I did not find peace. Quite the opposite, the only thing my foolish heart has brought me is scars from my disobedience to the Father, our Creator, and His Word.

I am so thankful for His mercy and the healing and restoration it brings when, in our brokenness and humility, we cry out for it. I promise, when we come to the end of ourselves and in our brokenness cry out for His mercy, He is faithful and "tends his flock like a shepherd: He gathers the lambs in his arms and carries them close to his heart" (Isaiah 40:11 NIV).

I continue to pray for you even from afar. I have asked the Father to draw you in close to His heart as we take a look at the beauty of the brokenness in Part Two of this chapter.

Part Two: The Beauty of Brokenness

Beauty: A meaningful design
Kindness. Joy. Laughter. Forgiveness. Creation. Love. Grace. Friendship. Healing.

Those are some of the words people used to describe beauty in a recent survey for this book. It is hard to marry those words to the idea of brokenness, isn't it? They are so opposite, the question begs to be asked, can there really be beauty in brokenness? Yes, there really can be! However, it is difficult to see it as beauty when everywhere we turn, we hear that broken is not good. Broken is worthless, and you don't have to settle for it.

During that same survey I asked the question, "What do you usually want to trade in your brokenness for?" I appreciated the realness and honesty in one woman's answer: "Perfection, healing, anything but brokenness." While she understood that perfection is impossible because we live in a broken world, she *can* attain healing from true effort and God's grace. However, she was being honest with where her emotions wanted to go. Again, there should be no guilt in our desiring and longing for what we were created: to be whole. The day is coming when all wrong will be made right again. Until then, be encouraged!

Healing is available right now, and beauty can be found in the middle of it all. But you must commit yourself to the process of healing. It won't be without effort. But it will be worth it. It is difficult not to get distracted from that truth: that it is available and worth it. It is difficult not to get discouraged from doing the difficult work when we hear that we don't even have to try to put the effort in mending what is broken, because there is always something better. In today's society, you can trade whatever is broken for something new that will make you *feel* happy again.

What we don't often hear about is that the cost of simply "trading in" is high, and emotions such as *happy* don't last. They are not supposed to. I often remember my grandpa saying, "Anything worth having would require work and effort." Yes, difficult work is, well, difficult to do. I don't enjoy the difficult work associated with my physical therapy or the pain that needs to be endured in hopes (with no guarantee) that it will make a difference. It is also difficult to remain committed to the discipline of doing my exercises at home when I am not being held accountable. It is tough when I am not being held accountable to managing my schedule in a way that allows me to keep what feels like an endless number of appointments. But unless I do it, there is no chance (never mind guarantee) that healing can happen. I also can't move to the next treatment unless I complete the first one. The muscles around my neck injury need to be strengthened before the next step can be taken. Is it worth it? Ask me when I am finished with my therapy. Yes! It is worth it. I know I will have done my part; therefore, I must trust God for the rest.

We have become a people of entitlements. We want fast results. It has become part of every marketing and advertising technique. "Want to lose weight fast? Just take this pill. No need to adjust your diet or do any kind of exercise." Anyone who experiences lasting results of good health will tell you that exercising and a lifestyle change of better eating are what will work. It requires commitment to doing the hard work. Ok. May I dig a little deeper? I don't think any of us will be surprised by it, but the next paragraph may sound a little bold or shocking. However, it must be addressed in order to transition from the *physical* to the *spiritual* conditioning of our hearts. How about this one: "Want to grow in your relationship with God and deepen your intimacy with Him? Join our study. We'll enjoy community and encourage each other. We know that life is busy. So, no worries, there is no homework involved with our study. Just come as you are." The reason I feel so passionate about that is because it justifies busyness instead of encouraging us to have quality time with God.

Yes, we should always come as we are. However, I don't know about you, but with me, it is easy to see when I am just trying to get by without putting in the effort or digging in deeper into His word and doing some homework. When I don't have quality time with God, my peace starts to fade as I quickly become distracted by the circumstances and busyness around me instead of resting in what I know to be true: His Word. Ok. I feel led to say this for all the wonderful rule-followers, how long do you set aside for your homework? That is between you and God. This has looked different throughout the different seasons in my life, and I have also been guilty of doing an in-depth study during the season of having small children and infants, while my husband was deployed, just so I could check my homework box. I don't recommend that either. God convicted me in that season that He was not impressed with my 40-minute in-depth study just to check that box. He was more interested in my heart. He would rather have 20 minutes of my heart being still in His Word than having my in-depth study homework box checked. So be it a season of stillness or in-depth studying, I have found that the only way to be able to remain at peace is by making time to dig in, study my Bible, keep my eyes on the truth, and yes, do my *homework,* but not just to check a box.

Sweet friend, here is what I have learned and am constantly reminded of: the depth of our peace will be measured by the depth of our relationship with God. And the depth of our relationship with God will always be a direct reflection of our time spent investing in it through quality not quantity time spent with Him, reading our Bibles, studying it, wrestling with the entire book of Romans or a short passage like 1 Thessalonians 5:16-18 and, most importantly, surrendering to it as the final authority in our lives and where our hearts will find peace. We just need to be committed to filling our hearts and our minds with His Word. Seek His Truth if you want to find lasting peace in your life.

> The depth of our peace will be measured by the depth of our relationship with God. And the depth of our relationship with God will always be a direct reflection of our time spent investing in it.

I promise, I understand that hard work is hard. I know that sometimes it would seem easier to run from the brokenness or fall into the "keep trading it in until you find what you want" mentality. I understand. I, too, have been guilty of wanting the pain and hurt that comes with brokenness to go away quickly. I have been guilty of running from emotion to emotion to get away from it. But when I have done that, it hasn't worked out very well.

I am reminded of a season in my life where I found myself running from the brokenness of a particular relationship, which was affecting many areas of my life. I knew that this relationship was not going to be a permanent one. There was a date in sight as to when it would come to an end. So I figured I would just "shove it all under the rug" and push through it. But I kept tripping over the lump under the rug. Why? Because the truth is that particular relationship was not the issue. Yes, interactions could have been different. However, what I was running from was the brokenness this particular relationship was bringing to the surface, and I could not get around it. It was one of those times that I kept trying to walk around it, dig under it, or jump over it, but God would not let go, and I kept tripping on it until I was willing to look at it.

So after all my running from it, I found myself having to *run* into a dressing room in the middle of the store I was at because in my running away from my brokenness, tears could no longer be held back. Try as I may to keep myself together, they wouldn't stop running down my face. I was reminded of a message I had gotten from a friend asking me to pray for her a while back. Her message read, "Gina! I've been digging this pit and realized that I belly flopped into it…bring a ladder, rope, anything and pray me out of here!" In that moment, when I realized that I too had been digging a pit and had belly flopped into it as I keep running from it, I finally cried out to my God saying, "Ok, Lord, here I am. Sitting on the floor of a dressing room! You win, you have my attention. That relationship is not the problem. My brokenness is. But it hurts too much! Why can't You just take it away?" I believe that, when

He hasn't just taken my pain away even when He could and sometimes does, He wants me to come to the end of myself in humility, with open hands and an open heart. He wants me to say, "Here it is, Lord! I give it to you. I surrender! Mercy!"

When I have done that, when I have surrendered to Him instead running away from my brokenness or staying stuck in the lie that "if only things were different," I have found the peace I was so desperately seeking. When I am still long enough while claiming His truth—be it in a dressing room at the store or sitting in front of the fireplace in my home—mercy comes running, picks me up, and dusts me off. And His peace, His everlasting peace, is restored once again in my life.

So as I sat on the floor of that fitting room, I sent a similar message to a friend, "Help! I have belly flopped into my own pit, please pray me back." She replied with a simple, "I'm on it." Her response was simple and short. It needed to be. In that moment of surrender, I needed for God to be the one who comforted me, not my friend. I needed to be still before Him and listen to His words. It was time to become unstuck and do the hard work of surrendering to my God, my Father, my Creator and not continue to allow His creation to define me. Yes, my journey back to peace started on the floor of a dressing room.

I don't know what causes you to be stuck thinking that if the circumstances in your life were different, you would find peace. I only can tell you why I get stuck. The reason I get stuck is because when I try to describe peace from where I stand, it is nothing like what I thought peace was before. To me, peace meant that everything had to be perfect without brokenness. Broken meant that I needed to either be able to fix it, be in deep pain from the agony of something being broken, or push aside the brokenness and go into survival mode...only to end up with unstoppable tears on the floor of a dressing room.

I shared in Chapter One that I grew up in what I know to be one of the most loving, giving, sacrificial Mexican families I know. Yes, we had our issues and dysfunction too, and we still do (who doesn't?). But issues, dysfunctions, craziness and all, there is one thing that is undeniable; it can't ever be said that we don't love each other.

One of the issues that my family and I have is that we don't always communicate well. I guess I forgot to mention "passionate" in my family's description. Yeah, we are that too, very much so. Why is it important to mention that we are passionate? Well, because it is important to understand some of our dysfunction. I still remember when a boyfriend, whom we will name Walter, joined my family and me for Christmas one year. At one point, Walter had a very perplexed look on his face. It reminded me of the look on Lucy Ricardo's face (from *I love Lucy*) when Ricky would lose it and start yelling at her in Spanish. So I asked Walter what was wrong. He replied with a simple question, "What in the world just happened?" Walter didn't speak Spanish. But he didn't have to in order to see that something was not right. You see, in moments of conflict, we are not always careful with our choice of words, and Walter just couldn't understand what he was witnessing as my family had one of those fine, passionate moments. To be honest, I am not sure any of us understand those moments other than it's the way it always has been.

It was Christmas Eve, and everyone was having a good time. But then I guess someone said something that was not well received by the other person, and a few not-so-well-chosen words started to be exchanged... passionately. Another important thing to know about my family is that we can quickly jump into each other's business without an invitation. Well, before Walter knew it, *everyone* got involved in that passionate moment, or as I lovingly refer to as "go all Mexican" on each other.

But that moment didn't last very long; they usually don't. My grandma jumped into the moment and finally said, "Enough! It's Christmas!" And just like that, everyone stopped, went back to having a good time, which we also do very well, and moved on. Everyone was back to laughing and hugging. Whatever the issue, it didn't get much attention until the next time it was passionately brought up after someone said something to trigger it back. This is what I call "sweep it under the rug until you trip over it again." I don't want to deal with my issues because they hurt too much. I just don't have the space to deal with them in my busy life. Just like when I landed on the dressing room floor because I kept tripping over the brokenness, and my identity was shaken by the circumstances in my life, I "sweep it under the rug until I trip over it again." So somehow, a dressing room floor ended up being the space in which God dealt with me.

Yes, I grew up in a family who, just like every other family, has issues and dysfunctions, but we genuinely care and love each other deeply. We really do. And for that I am thankful. Oh, and Walter, as wonderful of a guy as he was, did not end up being "the one." I did wonder a couple of times how much experiencing that moment with my family had to do with it.

However, you should know that up until about four years ago, you could not find a rug anywhere in my house, literally. Why? And what does that story about my family have to do with my quest for peace? I will need to dig a little deeper and share a vulnerable peace of my heart and a portion of my relationship with my dad with you in order to answer those questions.

Confession: my default is to leave my story at the surface level here. If I go any further, I risk being vulnerable which feels very, well, *vulnerable*. But there is freedom in vulnerability when done responsibly. And my wonderful editor won't let me just stop there. I keep finding review notes throughout my manuscript saying, "You need to expand a little more on that," or "You need to insert a personal example here," or "You need to be more vulnerable here so the reader understands." So, I have come to one of those review notes on the side of the margin here where I must expand and become vulnerable.

My dad experienced his first heart attack while my mom was five months pregnant with me. He was waterskiing, and my mom was driving the boat when she noticed something had gone terribly wrong. At five months pregnant, she jumped into the ocean to pull my dad out of the water and get him to the hospital as quickly as possible. By God's grace and my mom's effort, my dad survived that heart attack! As far as I can remember, my dad regularly told me that I was the reason he hadn't died that day. He often shared with me that he kept thinking he had to live so he could meet his baby, me. He often told me that I was the apple of his eye, and he treated me as such.

My parents divorced when I was only three years old. After the divorce and I had started school, one of my earliest memories was that of my dad stopping by the house on his way to work in the morning. Even though the school bus stop was less than half a block away, he would often pick me up, so we could drive around the block together before I got dropped off at the bus stop. He would smile and say, "Remember, you are what keeps me alive."

Then the second heart attack came. I don't remember how old I was or the details of it either. I do, however, remember getting to the hospital on time with the rest of my family. I remember going into his hospital room while he was still in critical condition. I went up to the bed and held his hand. I told him how afraid I was that he was going to die. As best as he could, he softly said, "Nothing to worry about. It will all be ok. Remember, you are what keeps me alive." Once again, he survived that heart attack.

One time I remember the doctor leaving after a home visit, telling my dad that he needed to watch what he ate, among other important advice. My sister, brother, and I lived with my mom, but my brother would stay at my dad's regularly. I didn't stay as regularly, but I often spent the night at my dad's. Well, it was one of the nights I said I would stay, but for some reason (to this day I don't remember why) I changed my mind, and I didn't stay the night. I have regretted that decision for many, many years. My dad suffered his third and final heart attack in the middle of that night. My poor brother found him dead in the morning when he went to kiss him on his way out the door for school. I can't even begin to imagine the horror that must have been for my brother. He was (and continues to be) one of the bravest men I know.

I remember the day perfectly; the school bell rang, and we walked into our classrooms. I was nine years old and in the fourth grade. Although my desk was close to the window, I could see the principal walking into the classroom. She said that I needed to gather my things and come to the office with her because my mom was waiting for me there. I will never—no, never—forget the ache my heart felt when my mom held me tight and struggled to find the words to tell me that my dad had died. I just kept saying, "No! It can't be!" over and over again. You see, it didn't make sense to me. I couldn't understand. He promised that he would never leave me. He told me time and time again that as long as I was here, he would be here, too, because I was what kept him alive! It didn't make sense. I didn't understand. If I kept him alive, why did he die?

Well, that moment was one of my first recollections of my trading in God's truth for a lie. The truth is, it wasn't my fault. The lie I picked up instead was that it was *my* fault. I was supposed to have been at his house that night. If I had been there, my dad would have survived that heart attack, and he would be alive today. That was the only thing that made sense to my nine year old brain, so I believed it and held tight to it.

The guilt and the shame I felt for not being there to save my dad from dying was such that I decided to not share it with anyone, not even my family who loved me and cared for me. So I stuffed it deep inside my soul instead. I guess you could say that "I swept it under the rug" and left it there for many years to come. I finally asked for help to deal with his loss in my late teens and young adult years after becoming a

Christian. I could no longer carry the burden. I could no longer deal with the nightmares that haunted me all those years. I was tired and weary of not being known for who I really was inside: a mess. But I had mastered the unhealthy art of "sweeping everything under the rug," and as far as everyone was concerned, I was doing just fine. But I really wasn't, and peace was nowhere to be found.

The only thing that could top the guilt and shame of not being there to keep my dad alive was not being able to protect my baby. By the time I was 21 years old, I had a baby in heaven. The brokenness from my helplessness only added to my "If I had only" collection of thoughts. The circumstances of my situation are extremely complicated, and at the time of sending this manuscript off to my publisher, I am not at liberty to share those details of my story. For all of us mommas (and dads) with a baby waiting for us in heaven, no matter the circumstance of losing a baby, the pain, the agony, the sleepless nights full of "what if's," can be more than one heart can bear at times. While the pain in the brokenness of having one of our babies (no matter the age) get to heaven before us never really goes away, you can find healing at the foot of Jesus' cross, and you can gain hope in His glorious resurrection. When my wondering, aching heart moments sneak up on me with the "what if's," I have to make a choice to be still before my God. In the stillness of that moment, while the circumstances and the brokenness that remain don't change, His mercy helps me find my way back to choosing peace…again.

At 21 years old I was also at the end of a marriage that I realized I couldn't save. I can still hear my ex-husband finally saying that I was not the girl he fell in love with anymore. As a result, I was no longer fun, and he didn't want to be married to me anymore. Yes, it was devastating to hear it, but the difficult part was that I couldn't argue with him about it anymore. The truth is, he was right. I wasn't the same girl anymore, and I was not able to change back to being "that girl" in hopes that he would love me again and would stay married to me. I know, this is coming from the girl who spent her life changing and transforming into whatever needed to be done in order to be accepted and avoid being abandoned. As difficult as it was to hear those words and as painful as it was to feel the failure of that marriage, nothing mattered anymore. In not so many words, I had been told that I was no longer good enough to be loved, and I was no longer worth fighting for. Yes, my brokenness was piling up (21 was not a good year for me).

My default would have been to change into whatever I needed to be in order to avoid failure and brokenness. But I no longer could go back to my default. You see, a new transformation had happened and permanent changes had started to take place. His name is Jesus! It was a couple of days after my 21st birthday that I had come to a "fork in the road." I had only been walking with Jesus for a short time, but the time had come. I had to make a decision. I was either going to believe that He was who He was or He wasn't. I would either take Him at His word as the only One who could promise to never leave me or believe the lie that He would one day abandon me, too.

Well, after everything, He delivered me from and all the times He kept His word, I chose *Him*. Not only did He think I was worth fighting for, but He proved I was worth dying for. Why am I worth Jesus' death on the cross? The same reason He knew *you* were worth dying for. Because I am His creation, just like you are. Because His heart breaks at the thought of spending eternity without us, His creation…Period! That, my sweet friend, is the only thing that will always be good enough. That is the only reason that when old or new brokenness comes my way, and I *choose* to be still before Him and trust Him for whatever outcome, I can finally get to a place where I can say, "It is well with my soul." It *is* all well with my soul, Lord. I will be still and know that *You* are my God.

Remember the "no rugs in my house" rule? That story about my family "sweeping it under the rug" has a lot to do with my quest for peace. I want to share another piece of my heart with you. (And I am choosing to do this before I get that lovely review note from my editor on the side of the margin this time!) The story of my family simply helps to paint a picture of what my default used to be when the pain and conflict of brokenness came my way. When conflict would arise and the brokenness hurt more than I could bear, instead of being still and allowing God to clean out my wounds, I would push back and say, "Not yet, God! It still hurts too much! Not yet!" And I would "sweep it under the rug" and leave it there. It worked, until something else came my way or until someone else would say something that would trigger my brokenness, and I would trip over it again.

So, about twenty years ago, I made the decision that I literally didn't want any rugs wherever I lived. I had entered a season of starting to understand myself better, and in order to embrace the brokenness, it would need to be kept from going back under the rug when the pain was more than I could bear. The "no rugs rule" would serve as a reminder that my home would be a safe place, and I could keep things in the open between me and God. I didn't want to play any more "sweep it under the rug" games with God. It was time for the healing to begin. It was time to embark on a life long journey of choosing peace in the midst of the brokenness.

I need to share more with you on the rug situation in our home. It was about four years ago that our family was getting ready to move to our dream home. A dear and wiser-than-me friend was over. We were sitting at the kitchen table when I was sharing with her why we didn't have rugs in the house. She turned to me and said, "Gina, you know, rugs are not the problem. You just need to make sure that you sweep or vacuum under them every once in a while." Ha! There is so much wisdom in that statement.

Sometime later when we had finally completed our move to the new house, another dear and wiser-than-me friend had come over so I could show her the new house. As we were standing by the fireplace in our living room with some beautifully and freshly stained and sealed wood floors, she said, "This would be a great place for a beautiful rug." I chuckled and said, "We'll see." She is familiar with my "no rug rule." As we were leaving the living room, she said, "You do know that rugs warm up a room, right? They also provide soft landings in hard places." There is so much wisdom in that statement, too! I guess that is why they are both my wiser-than-me friends.

The update on my "no rugs in the house rule" is that we now have seven rugs throughout our home. And yes, they have provided warmth in cold seasons and soft landings in hard places. I just make it a point to sweep or vacuum under them when it's time for some deep cleaning around the house. The rugs now serve as a beautiful reminder of God's grace and mercy in my life and the fact that He will forever remain the God who never leaves me and who walks with me "in the cool of day" even if it is a frozen winter here in this beautiful state of Michigan.

"Mercy" by Matt Redman runs through my heart when I look back in my life, reminding me of God's mercy: "I will kneel in the dust, at the foot of the cross where mercy paid for me…May I never lose the wonder, oh the wonder of Your mercy. May I sing Your hallelujahs, hallelujah amen." Finding peace will require our humility before Almighty God. Peace will require our kneeling down at the foot of the cross and being still while trusting Him for the rest.

So, if we know that His peace is what we are longing for, and we now know how to find it, why is it such a struggle? Because pride, the opposite of humility, gets in the way. The truth is that pride and humility are not just opposite of each other; they repel each other! They simply cannot co-exist, and humility is required for us to kneel at the foot of the cross. I understand that pride is not always bad in the proper context. However, it has the potential to be deadly when not kept in check.

There are different types of pride, and I understand that not all pride is bad. In Genesis 3, we find arrogant pride, but throughout other scriptures, pride is not always arrogant. Much like Adam and Eve, you and I think we may have a better plan, a better way than God, and we act on it because we think God is just holding out on us. No, the good pride we must have is best recorded when God the Father says, "This is my Son, whom I love; with Him I am well pleased" (Matthew 3:17), or when we read about Jesus teaching the Parable of The Talents: "Well done, good and faithful servant. You have been faithful over a little; I will set you over much. Enter into the joy of your Master" (Matthew 25:21).

You and I may not always be arrogantly prideful. But I am sure we've all had our moments. I know I have. Those moments of arrogant pride for me (which is the kind that I will keep making reference to) have looked different throughout the various stages in my life.

Prior to coming to Jesus, my pride looked something like, "You didn't rescue me back then. You didn't care to answer my prayers. Why would I even bother to cry out and trust You now?" Today as I look back over my life—even through some of my most broken and painful moments—I can see that He was *always* there. But why couldn't I see it then? Pride kept me from seeing it because life didn't look the way *I* wanted it to look. It didn't look the way *I* thought it should. It had not gone according to my *better* plan. My dad died, I had a baby in heaven, and I had a failed marriage. My times of abandonment from failing to change and please others enough had become too many to count. As a result, when I made bad choices, I blamed God for the consequences of my sin and the choices I had made. After all, if brokenness had not come my way, I would not have ended up making some of those bad choices. As far as I was concerned, it was all God's fault; I was not assuming responsibility for my choices. As you can see, peace was not the only thing I couldn't find. Humility was absent, too.

Pride looked a little different after I surrendered my life to Jesus. It was more difficult to identify this pride because it looked like something *good.* It looked a lot like *extreme* humility. I say "extreme" because there is a difference. Extreme humility is when you hear people say things like, "I am so unworthy. I don't deserve anything." And they get stuck there. Extreme humility is what lands us belly flopping in our own pity party pit. The truth is that humility does not have the need to be extreme. Humility is all it needs to be on its own. Nothing less, nothing more. Sweet friend, extreme humility is just the other side of pride. And it is just as ugly, because they both take the focus away from God and back on us.

May I dig a little deeper? Pride can also manifest itself when we compare ourselves and our stories with others. When people say, "But I don't have a dramatic story of giving my life to Jesus." My answer is, "Great! Praise Him for it! You have your own story of redemption." You don't need someone else's story to tell. You have your own! Listen closely here, sweet friend, no one can tell your story the way you can, and you are not supposed to tell anyone else's story. The focus should never be on our stories. The focus should always—and only—be on what God has done through the redemption of our broken lives.

Our stories are supposed to be different to reach different people for His kingdom. Some of the brokenness in our stories comes from our own choices and past failures. Some of our brokenness was caused by the choices of others, leaving us marked with pain and sadness. We should never compare our brokenness to each other because at the end of the day, the same grace that has pulled some of us out of our belly flopping pits of destruction and despair is what has kept others from digging and belly flopping into their own pits. It is not about you, me, or our stories. It's about Him being glorified through every circumstance. The truth is we don't always need to be rescued from a train wreck in order to have a story that is dramatic enough for Him to be glorified. When we compare our stories, pride is front and center. When pride compares, one story becomes more glorified than another, and we get lost in worshiping *our stories* instead of God. The truth is this: broken is broken, and pain is pain. Your story has everything needed to tell God's story as long as He is the center of it. Always remember this: God is most glorified through the surrender of our pride when in humility we give Him the glory.

My hope is that part one of this chapter has brought clarity to how quickly we can have a distorted view of God and why sin has brought brokenness into the world. Remember I said before that we should not be too hard on Adam and Eve? Yeah, we can do the same thing they did when our pride gets in the way.

Another way our pride sneaks in and our peace starts to fade is when we allow the roles God has entrusted us with throughout the different seasons in our lives to define us. Let me explain; if you are single, the frequently asked question is, "Are you dating someone?" If you are dating, it turns into, "Are you two serious?" or "When are you two getting married?" As if being single is a disease of some sort. But, don't feel bad, my amazing single friends. It's not just singles the world picks on. You are not alone. The expectations move right into the next season. When the wedding finally comes, the question almost immediately turns into, "So, when are you going to have kids?"

When the wedding finally comes it can often be accompanied by "Yay! Welcome to the club." We spend much of our time comparing ourselves to the other club members and wonder if we will measure up as a wife. Then those beautiful, amazing, and most wonderful babies come along next and change *everything*, and life as you know it gets turned upside down in the most beautiful and scary way possible. In the middle of the sleep deprivation, someone asks if the baby is sleeping through the night yet, and you wonder if you are doing something wrong because they are not. And when the sleep deprivation comes to an end (even though you never really sleep well again because you are now walking around with your heart outside of your body), we find ourselves comparing our children to what others are doing, how many awards they are getting in school or how many sports they are playing. We start measuring our success by what others might think of our children. And yes, before we know it, pride—not the good kind—sneaks in and our contentment slips away, along with our peace.

Oh, I wish I could tell you that the crisis ends there. Well, it actually could. But unfortunately, if we don't catch ourselves, the crisis can go on until it all comes to an explosion during the dreaded mid-life crisis we always hear about. I honestly think I just went through the first wave of mine when I turned 40 a couple of years ago. It was that year when I finally threw my hands up in the air and said, "I don't care what label you want to put on me! No, I don't have it all together. I am broken just like everyone else!"

I too have plenty of insecurities I must keep in check, and I often wonder if I measure up. Yes, my life can get messy! But broken, with my insecurities, messy life and all, I remain a daughter of Almighty God. I will walk, crawl, run, dance, and jump in that truth! It is only at that moment of surrender and letting go of our pride as we humble ourselves before God that we find freedom to just *be*. We can finally start getting comfortable in our own skin. I am not talking about freedom to do whatever we want just because His grace covers it all, and mercy is available. No, I am talking about the freedom in knowing *Whose we are* and therefore knowing *who we are*. We have freedom in knowing that "But by the grace of God I am what I am, and his grace to me was not without effect" (1 Corinthians 15:10). Yes, it is hard to come to the end of ourselves to trade our pride for humility. But that trade-in always works, and I promise, humility is always worth it.

It is worth it. Trading our pride for humility will prepare our hearts for when the brokenness of a relationship we'd hope would end our singleness comes to an end, and the disappointment and hurt is ever so real. Humility will help us to cry out, "Lord, mercy! I am Yours! It hurts but continue to refine me, so that if it is Your will, You may present me to my mate as Your radiant bride. Your will be done, Lord, not mine. This brokenness is Yours, Lord! I will trust in You!"

When we trade our pride for humility, humility will prepare our hearts for when the wonderful man we love and get to share our lives with comes along and, in our brokenness, we hurt each other deeply. When the fires in our marriages break out, as they do, instead of running towards the fire escape, we need humility to own our brokenness, to put our heads together so that our marriages are not consumed by the fire, but instead refined by it. And, when we feel alone in the fight, and—trust me when I tell you that both my man and I have felt that way at one point or another in our marriage—it is so very difficult to put our needs aside when the emotion is real and the wound a bit raw. In those moments, it will require humility to cry out, "Lord! Mercy! I surrender! This broken marriage is yours. Do whatever it takes...and yes, start with me!"

Surrendering will require trading in our pride for humility when—after reading many parenting books, blog posts, Facebook posts, and more about how to be a great parent—we still find ourselves at a loss for what to do with these beautiful children He has trusted us to raise for His kingdom. It will require humility to cry out, "Lord! Mercy! I don't know how to do this, but You have trusted us with these children, and with them I know You will give us the wisdom, patience, and endurance that is needed to raise them for Your glory. These wonderfully broken children are Yours, Lord. Mercy!"

And, oh, when some of our long awaited dreams take an unexpected turn; when in our limited understanding our dreams appear to have died; when the fire and passion in our hearts starts to fade because we just don't understand; when we grow weary; when temptation creeps in for us to give in to whatever temptation the apple represents—it will require humility to come to the end of ourselves and cry out, "I don't know how to do this, Lord! But I only want Your dreams for me. I lay it all down. I surrender, Your will be done. These dreams are Yours…Mercy!"

None of this is ever easy, and it's often accompanied by an ugly cry, the kind of cry where we have to catch our breath and wipe the tears off our keyboard as we type. I understand those ugly cries. They have been the kind of ugly cries that make me want to say, "Enough! This hurts too much" and default back to "shoving it under the rug" moments. Yes, the hard work is hard to do. But please take heart! Let me encourage you here. The day comes when the tears hitting the keyboard (like mine are right now), are a result of the greatness of His faithfulness. Take heart! Yes, it hurts, and it may take a little bit for you to catch your breath. But here is the beautiful thing, if your tears at that moment are ones of brokenness, the victory can be yours, too. But we must first trade in the lie for His truth and hold on with all we have to the promises found in His Word. We often want to just get to the promise of Jeremiah 29:11. We want Him to tell us the great plans He has for our lives—ones full of hope for a great future. Yet the Bible tells us in Jeremiah 29:13 that He will be found when we seek Him with *all our hearts*. Not just parts of it, *all* of it. Don't run from the hurt and shove it under the rug. Take heart…there is always hope, even in the pain and brokenness.

So, after all of that, where is the beauty in brokenness? The beauty is in those moments of surrender where we are reminded that God, the creator of the universe, *our* Creator still specializes in bringing back to life that which is dead. Oh, and when He does, scoot over!

Listen, you know you've heard it said, "God showed up." I used to say the same thing. I understand and fully appreciate the sentiment in which that is often spoken by

> The beauty is in those moments of surrender where we are reminded that God, the creator of the universe, *our* Creator still specializes in bringing back to life that which is dead.

fellow brothers and sisters in Christ. However, the theology of that statement is way off. Why? Because God doesn't ever have to show up. He is already there! He is simply waiting for *us* to show up. Because when we finally *do* show up, when in our brokenness we finally come to the end of ourselves and surrender, then He has a way of showing *off!* Through the beauty of brokenness and humility, we find our way to peace as we cry out to God for His mercy. When we do that, He shows off by doing "immeasurably more than all we ask or imagine, according to His power that is at work within us" (Ephesians 3:20 NIV). That is a beautiful thing.

No, brokenness is not easy and it does not *feel* good. Humility is not easy either as it requires the laying down of our pride. Surrender is a foreign word to many of us because it represents weakness. Yet, there is beauty in it all. In part, that beauty is its reminder to us of our desperate need for God.

Exercise

What areas of your life are broken?

What is your default in dealing with that brokenness?

What does quality time with God looks like in your life?

How does pride (not the good kind) manifest in your life? What triggers it?

When was the last time you swept "under the rug" and what did you find?

Write a response to God with what He has revealed to you. Acknowledge your brokenness and find the beauty of thankfulness for all He has done in your life.

Chapter Three

Choosing Peace

I am not sure how many of you remember the "Y2K crisis." It was the warning that alerted the world that if computer systems were not upgraded and adapted to accommodate dates switching from the 20th Century to the 21st Century (year 1999 to year 2000) it could cause catastrophic failure to computer systems around the world. Companies that took the warning seriously and updated their systems did not experience the "crash" expected. They were successful in having a smooth transition into the year 2000. Some of the companies that did nothing about the warning suffered pretty harsh consequences. In many cases, those companies had a very difficult time recovering from the Y2K crash, and some never recovered at all.

So what in the world does Y2K have to do with peace? Nothing, really. Except that it reminded me of the difference between listening to the warning that can have catastrophic consequences in our lives and what happens when we ignore those warnings. It reminded me of the difference between choosing to make the adjustments necessary to remain at peace or ignoring the brokenness.

No, I didn't experience any consequences of the crash of Y2K, but unfortunately I have experienced the consequences and the brokenness that comes when I have ignored (sometimes intentionally and sometimes not) that gentle whisper from the Holy Spirit warning me that a new season was coming. I have experienced the brokenness that results from being distracted with the busyness of *doing* some really good things for God instead of *being* available for God in my hope to avoid the brokenness.

We can quickly lose our peace when we allow the noise of busyness to drown that gentle whisper that says, "Pay attention. The weather is changing, and the storm is on its way .You will need to adjust and 'update your systems' if you don't want to 'crash'. Make room in your schedule, and stay as close to me as possible." When you listen to that warning, you choose peace in the storm and the brokenness it brings.

No, Y2K was not the year that required adapting or adjusting my "systems," which for me, translates to my schedule. The year 2000 for the most part was a pretty great year actually. However, it wasn't that long ago that our family experienced the biggest transition we've had to walked through when my man retired from the Marine Corps after 25 years of service. We were used to transitioning every three years or so when the next set of orders came. And we were used to moving and could turn a house into a home in no time. We didn't necessarily love having to transition, but we knew it was a regular part of our lives, and we always looked forward to the next adventure. My man loved being a Marine, and I considered it an honor to be a Marine's wife. But we both knew that it was time to leave the Corps, and we were at peace with the decision of his retirement.

Because transitioning was what we were used to, when it came time to transition into life outside of the military, we didn't think a lot about it. Yes, we made sure that every major box on the list was checked, and all the major things were in order. We moved into our dream home with much help from friends.

When we moved into the new house, we knew that we had a lot of work to do in order to make this dream house our own. (We are still working on it four years later!) We knew there would be *a lot* of boxes that we would need to go through and things to get rid of as we were finally in our "forever home." We no longer had to keep things just in case we needed them for the next house. Yes, we knew all of that. And for the most part, just like every time before, the house was turned into our home rather quickly.

Once the house was set up, and we started to get comfortable, life was good. Then one day I was having a conversation with the wife of a Marine who had just retired, and she casually asked if we were getting settled in the house. "Yes," I said. "Well, you know, the kitchen is unpacked, the rooms are set up, and pictures are hanging on the wall. We are pretty much unpacked except—," and she interrupted me and finished my sentence for me: "—except the boxes that you have been moving around for years that you don't even know what is in them anymore." *Yes!* That is exactly it. But to be honest, I am not really looking forward to that process." She smiled and said, "Yeah, I understand. I have those boxes, too."

I believe that was the first "whisper" that I recall from God, "Pay attention. The weather is changing, and the storm, along with the sifting is on its way. You will need to adjust and 'update your systems' if you don't want to 'crash.' You will need to make room in your schedule and choose to stay as close to me as possible. If you do that, you will be choosing peace in the storm ahead and the brokenness it will bring."

I need to share that it wasn't all about the physical boxes that needed to be unpacked. Yes, they would require sifting through in order to see what would stay and what needed to go. And while I ended up getting rid of 90% of the contents in those boxes (because I hadn't needed them in years), I was so glad I didn't just toss them out. During the sorting process, I found a treasured box inside one of them with some pictures I thought had been lost in a move as well as love letters I had received from my man during deployment.

This process wasn't about the physical boxes at all. It was about the "boxes" that needed to be unpacked in the storage room of my heart. You know, those "boxes" that we realize we don't have the time or space to "unpack," so we save them for later? Yeah, those boxes. While digging through the physical boxes in our storage room at home was no fun task, the boxes I was finding in my heart were the ones I was having a harder time unpacking. There were only a few boxes but they weren't easy ones. They were the boxes that we don't really want to look into because even though they have our name on them, we are not even sure what we will find in them. Yeah, those are the boxes I am talking about. There weren't many of them, but each one held a label that was dear to my heart. Without realizing it, in the craziness of all the transitions, I had allowed these labels to hold a grip on my identity: wife, mom, leader, daughter, sister, and friend.

Each move, I glanced at the boxes and would tell myself that they were not that big of a deal and that they could wait. After all there weren't many of them. But every once in a while, I was reminded that those boxes were still there. They would remind me that I needed to make adjustments and "update my system" so that I could unpack these boxes in my heart. But I kept thinking, "There is no time, Lord! Look at all the things I have on my schedule for *you*! I am homeschooling the kids. I am leading a ministry. I am trying hard to be a good friend to others. We are hosting a small group in our home. I am running around in between all the kids' activities. I am back in school pursuing Biblical Studies." And so on.

Please don't be impressed by any of that. God wasn't impressed by my long list of good things. His response was simple, "I know you are doing it all for me. But I have a question for you: What have I asked you to do?" Did He really just ask me that? Did He really just call me out? Yes, He most certainly did. I knew exactly what He was talking about. But I also knew that in order for me to take my next step with Him, those "boxes" in my heart would need to be unpacked. I now had a choice to make as old and new brokenness started to come to the surface as one by one each of those "boxes" in my heart would start to burst open under the pressure of unmet expectations, setting up the perfect storm for that identity crisis I found myself in. I had a choice to make. Would I continue to be distracted with the busyness of my long list of good things? Or would I choose peace in the brokenness by adjusting my "systems" and getting back to His feet, staying there long enough to be still?

Is peace really something that must be chosen? The answer is *yes*! And the beauty of peace is that it's a choice readily available for us to make. Just like our brokenness doesn't look the same, we may choose peace differently, but in order for us to be able to have lasting peace, peace must be chosen

Join me in looking at what choosing peace looks like as we journey through the story of two sisters, Martha and Mary. We first find the sisters hosting Jesus and the twelve disciples in their home without an RSVP or much notice of the men's arrival. It is a short passage without many details. However, it holds an amazing lesson in our quest for peace and how achieving it requires a choice. As with these two sisters, our choices determine if we end up with peace or anxiety in the brokenness.

Martha and Mary
Now as they went on their way, Jesus entered a village. And a woman named Martha welcomed him into her house. And she had a sister called Mary, who sat at the Lord's feet and listened to his teaching. But Martha was distracted with much serving. And she went up to him and said, "Lord, do you not care that my sister has left me to serve alone? Tell her then to help me." But the Lord answered her, "Martha, Martha, you are anxious and troubled about many things, but one thing is necessary. Mary has chosen the good portion, which will not be taken away from her." Luke 10:38–42

We have probably all related to one or both sides of this story at one point in our lives. We can often relate to the "Martha-working-hard" part, sometimes to the point that we get lost in the business of the task before us and forget to get back to the feet of Jesus, or what I like to call "a position of Mary." We can often get so concerned with "doing life" that we quickly lose sight of who we are serving and what our purpose is. Yes, the doing is important; however, at some point we must be willing to lay down and surrender whatever is needed to get back to the position of Mary and say, "Lord, I have done my part. I am here. Now have Your way in me."

Then we have Mary's side of the story. We don't know how she ended up at the feet of Jesus in this passage. We only know that at the point where Luke shares the story of the sisters, Mary is already at His feet instead of helping her sister Martha, who is clearly upset with her.

Sitting at the feet of Jesus was a place where you would find the disciples. During this time and in this culture, a woman sitting at the feet of the Rabbi was frowned upon. Why is this important to keep in mind? Because she didn't care about the expectations the world or her culture had of her. We shouldn't care about those expectations either. There is no peace in trying to please the world or our culture. Mary chose "the good portion" at the risk of inviting scorn for violating a cultural norm as well as the frustration of her sister, Martha. Yet, Jesus said that "the good portion" would not be taken from Mary. What I am saying is that we follow Jesus and no one else. I am saying that we can't let our culture or this broken world we live in define us. Mary didn't. If we are going to find peace, His word must be the final authority in our lives, and, therefore, we submit to it.

I am not sure about you, but before I began digging into this passage, whenever I looked at this story of the sisters, I often had the feeling that Martha got a bad rep for being busy, and Mary, as the positive example, got picked on for being the goody two-shoes and sitting at Jesus' feet.

Our preconceived notions of this story lead us to believe that Martha was doing something wrong. But Jesus didn't say that. He didn't tell Martha that her serving was a bad thing. What He pointed out was that Mary had chosen the good portion, and it would not be taken away from her. I'd like to think that instead of one sister being better than the other, they both struggled and made mistakes, like all of us, but made good choices, too. In this passage, it is clear that Mary chose the better way.

In Martha's defense, she is the one mainly focused on the task. The passage begins with her being the one who welcomed Jesus into their home. It would appear Martha was the one who pulled out her apron and took the initiative of the planning that would come with hosting Jesus and the disciples at a moment's notice. That would lead me to believe that she had space in her life to be available for Jesus and was not always anxious or distracted. It requires order and availability to be able to open your home like that at a moment's notice. We can see her heart starts out in the right place and in the truest meaning of servanthood. After all, she is the one running around the kitchen making sure everyone is getting what they need. Yet at some point, she becomes distracted and loses her focus. Instead of serving Jesus, her focus turns to all that needs to be done and the lack of support from her sister. She takes her eyes off of Jesus, and in doing so, she gets frustrated with Mary.

Speaking of Mary, I still get a good laugh when I think of the day I first wondered how Mary got to the feet of Jesus. I had read the story many times but had never contemplated this before. Perhaps it didn't become clear to me until I was at that point of needing to unpack the boxes in my heart. Because I was having a difficult time finding my way back to that position of Mary, I was desperately longing to sit at Jesus' feet. Like Martha, I had become distracted by *doing* and by the anxiety that comes when I focus a little too much on the task; I neglect making room in my life to be at His feet. I was running on a "15 minute shot of Jesus" in the morning and expecting it to be enough to keep my priorities in order. I expected this quick devotion to keep my "boxes" from exploding. The funny thing is that I was spending an incredible amount of time in the Scriptures because I was in the midst of getting a Biblical Studies Certification from Liberty University. However, I was having a hard time allowing what I was learning to find its way from my head to my heart. That would require me to stop the busyness in order to have time to just be at His feet. Yes, it had been a season that started with all the right intentions and for all the right reasons. However, just like Martha, I, too, had become distracted.

It was a Sunday morning, and the teaching was on the two sisters when our pastor pointed out that Scripture doesn't tell us how Mary got to Jesus' feet. The story starts with her already there. All of a sudden my brain spun in a hundred different directions thinking, "Hmm, true. Hmm, how in the world did she get there?" I turned to my man and quietly asked him, "So, how did she get there?" To which he gently put his arm around me and replied with a cute smirk on his face, "Scripture does not say. Are you paying attention?" Okay, confession: I wasn't paying attention because I couldn't let it go. I wish I could tell you that after all the digging into my books and commentaries on the passage I found something. But I didn't. We don't know how Mary gets to Jesus' feet in this story. She is just there.

Now, buckle up and join me in a short journey of "Hmm, what if?" I think that occasionally God leaves an answer out of the Bible just so we take the time to ponder the possibilities. It can be a good exercise for our souls as long as we are careful not to stray from established doctrine. So, what if? What if Mary, up until that point, had been running around like Martha? What if she, much like what I was feeling, was running on empty? What if, like me, she didn't really even know what she was missing or how to find her way to it? Yet, she knew she needed something. What if all of a sudden Mary recognizes what it is she needs when she sees Jesus walking in the room, and she sees peace? Hmm, Mary, much like I did now, has a choice to make. Does she stay to simply fulfill her duties or does she risk some controversy (and conflict) to get back to peace? Does she lay it all down, not caring that her brokenness will be known or what anyone would think of her? Now that she has been made aware of her need, does she let her pride get in the way or with humbleness does she *choose* the good portion? Well, her *choice* is more than clear in Scripture. She *chooses* to sit at the feet of Jesus. She *chooses* the good portion and trusts Him to take care of the rest. In doing so, she chooses peace as she sits at His feet, carefully listening to every word He is saying.

That moment was a game changer for me. It was what I call a "ding-ding-ding moment" for me getting back to that position of Mary, getting back to unpacking those boxes in my heart, and in doing so, getting back to peace. You know, it's those moments when the light finally goes on and all the dots connect. Yes, it was then that I realized I had allowed good and well intended things to bring confusion and distraction from what really matters. Sweet friend, if you get nothing else from this chapter, get this: Regardless of what you are currently doing in life, be it working or serving, no matter the season of life you find yourself in—single, friend, daughter, wife, or mom—what really matters is choosing the good portion right where we are. It is the one requirement to peace. It is the only place in which we are reminded that, yes, our brokenness will remain until Jesus returns or calls us home. But broken and all, we remain deeply loved by the only One who can love us best and make us whole. It's a journey, and it takes time. But it is *so* worth it. We will talk about that journey in the next chapter. We first have a choice to make!

That's where I was, at the point of having to choose. It had been a season in my life that, like Martha, it had started with all the right intentions for the right reasons. It had been a season in which I got to see God do some incredible things as He would move in ways only He could move in my personal life and in ministry. God had opened some doors that I didn't even know I wanted to open, or maybe I just didn't dare dream that He would even open these doors for me. Unfortunately, it later became a season in which, like Martha, I got distracted by the expectations I allowed others to put on me and the expectations I put on myself. I allowed the labels in my boxes to mess with my identity. And as a result, like Martha, I found myself distracted, exhausted, and frustrated. I found myself in a bit of that identity crisis we struggle with when either old or new brokenness rises to the surface. It was in that moment that I realized peace was available, but like Mary, peace needed to be *chosen* by getting back to that position of Mary and sitting at the feet of Jesus. My question of how she got to the feet of Jesus no longer mattered. I just needed to get there.

My opportunity to get on my knees and at the feet of Jesus came quickly after that Sunday morning. It was during one of my driest and most tired days. I had been running on empty for a bit, and it showed. I was looking for a scripture that I needed the reference to as I was wrapping up a final paper for one of my Old Testament classes when I found myself in the Gospel of Luke. Remember, I was supposed to be in the Old Testament! That is how distracted and tired I was when God showed me the following scripture. I had seen the verse before, but this time it made my heart tremble as He was speaking right to my heart.

I read, "Behold, Satan demanded to have you, that he might sift you like wheat" (Luke 22:31). Ah! How I wish to tell you that because I had heard (not listened to) the whisper that "the sifting was coming" my response was graceful, humbled and not so self-centered. However, my response can be summed up with, "Wait!!! But you said 'no,' right? Please? Lord, I am so tired. I am so dry. I am not sure that in my dryness I won't break. You said 'no,' right? Please?" Yes, I know it sounds like pleading, because it was! His response did include a "but." Just not the one I wanted, or the one I thought I needed. However, it was the "but" I desperately needed in order to lay down every piece of my brokenness at the foot of the cross and humbly cry out, "Lord Jesus, Mercy! I can't carry this anymore. I am tired, and I am dry. Here I am; take the pieces of my brokenness, and use it for your glory. I surrender! I can't carry the weight of the unmet expectations anymore. No. You haven't called me to teach women how to be a perfect wife so they can have the perfect marriage. I know that because I am not perfect, and as wonderful as my marriage is, I don't have a perfect one. You haven't called me to teach women how to be the perfect mom so they can have perfect kids, because I am not one and as much as I adore my kids, I don't have perfect kids. You have not called me to teach women how to be the perfect ministry leader so they can have a perfect ministry because I am not one, and I don't lead perfectly. You haven't asked me to be the perfect friend, because I am not one, and I can say and do some really stupid things from time to time. I surrender! Help me to get back to Your feet, and in doing so, help me find my way back to peace. I choose You, Lord! I choose the better portion. Here I am, Lord! Let the sifting begin." Surrendering wasn't easy, and it hurt. However, I was finally at peace.

The "but" I desperately needed was found in the very next verse when Jesus says, "but I have prayed for you that your faith may not fail. And when you have turned again, strengthen your brothers [and sisters]" (Luke 22:32). Two things in that verse have captured my heart in a brand new way. When we are so tired and dry, when we don't know how things will play out, when every area that is near and dear to our hearts ends up being sifted as we start unpacking our boxes, He prays for us a very specific prayer, that whatever we find in those boxes, our faith may not fail us. And He does it for a very specific purpose "when you have turned again, strengthen your brothers [and sisters]." Oh, there is so much hope in that verse when we take the time to look at it and hold on to the promise: the promise that none of our pain, struggles, or tears are ever wasted. The promise that there will be a turning point and that when the turning point comes, in His mercy He will use it all to encourage others. That is what He has called all of us to do: encourage others. By doing so, He brings glory to His name and the advancement of His kingdom. The beautiful promise that through it all, on the mountain tops as well as in the deepest of valleys, He remains God, the God who never leaves us and who never lets go of us.

Now, hear me out. While I would not have asked for that verse when He gave it to me or the sifting that came with it, it was during the sifting of my heart that I needed to be reminded of this: just like Martha, we can be distracted with good things and become anxious, yet only one thing is required— our humble and desperate need of Him. Our brokenness is the

Our brokenness is the beautiful reminder that the intimacy and peace Mary had with Jesus is available to every single one of us. Only one thing is required: to get back to a position of Mary and *choose* the good portion.

beautiful reminder that the intimacy and peace Mary had with Jesus is available to every single one of us. Only one thing is required: to get back to a position of Mary and *choose* the good portion.

No, Jesus didn't say that what Martha was doing was wrong. We all know that there is much to be done for the Kingdom, and everyone's capacity is different. But we must be careful not to keep adding side dishes in order to keep up with the busyness, demands, or expectations. We must make it a point to remain *available to Him* instead of being *busy for Him*, and we can only do that by spending time at His feet. We must go through our "boxes," asking Him what needs to go and what gets to stay, before the boxes starts to burst out open!

We find the sisters next in John 11:1–46. This passage is a bit longer and with a lot more detail. I highly encourage you to make time to read it. For now, let's journey through some key points.

Martha and Mary had sent word to Jesus that their brother Lazarus was very ill. By the time Jesus gets there, Lazarus had been dead four days. In this case, when they get news that Jesus is on His way, Martha is the one who goes out to meet Him while Mary stayed in the house mourning. While Martha's greeting is not the most gracious one, it gives us a glimpse into the realness of her relationship with Jesus. In not so many words, her greeting is, "What took you so long?"

Interestingly enough, Jesus does not feel the need to explain Himself or apologize for His delay. He gives her hope by assuring her that Lazarus will rise. Make no mistake here; Martha's faith has not failed her as she believes that, even though her brother is dead, there is something that Jesus can do. She believes that her brother will rise in the resurrection on the last day. Yes, she believes. Yet, in the rawness of her pain, she wants to know what about this pain right now? If Jesus knew of Lazarus' sickness and could have prevented his death, why didn't he come sooner? We could again give Martha a hard time here. But one of the things that

I have come to love about Martha is that she is just as intimate with Jesus as Mary is. Her intimacy with Him just looks different. We can see that she is secure enough in their relationship to ask Him the questions we all want answers to in the rawness of the moment. Jesus does not ignore her pain, but in gentleness reminds her to whom she is speaking and tells her that He is "the resurrection and the life." Her response changes and takes a more humble tone when she says, "Yes, Lord; I believe that you are the Christ, the Son of God..." (v.27).

Meanwhile, Mary is inconsolably broken inside the house. She is probably wondering where Jesus is in the midst of all this pain, too. Does He even care? Did He forget about us? She was probably grieved and disappointed that Jesus didn't get there sooner. Even though she believed that Jesus could have done something prior to Lazarus dying, her hope now seemed a little overshadowed by the death right before her eyes. However, unlike our previous passage, this time we do know how she gets to the feet of Jesus. Martha, the sister who previously complained about her being at His feet comes to get her and lets her know that Jesus is asking for her. While still in her pain, she responds to His calling and quickly gets up, and we read that, "When Mary came to where Jesus was and saw Him, she fell at his feet saying to him, "Lord, if you had been here, my brother would not have died" (v.32). Jesus once again does not feel the need to explain Himself or give apologies for his timing. That does not mean that He didn't care. We read that as He sees their pain and brokenness, He was deeply moved and that "He wept" (v.35).

They made their way to the place where the sisters had buried Lazarus. By this time there are many other witnesses along with them. Jesus asks for the stone to be removed. While still not understanding, they choose to trust Jesus when he tells Martha, "Did I not tell you that if you believed you would see the glory of God?" (v.40). He prays to the Father and calls out Lazarus from the grave. Lazarus comes out, and many of the witnesses that came with them believed in Him when they saw Jesus raise Lazarus from the dead.

Wow! There is so much packed in there. Talk about God showing off in a marvelous way. However, I wonder if anyone in the crowd (or reading this passage) asked themselves, "Hmm, but could He have done it differently? Could He have come and healed Lazarus while He was alive? Could He have spared them of all that pain?" The answer to the questions is "yes." However, He chooses to raise up Lazarus in a way that will bring all the glory to the Father while also stretching and growing our faith.

I am sure that while the sisters would not have chosen this route and all the brokenness that came with it, now they get a glimpse into the full picture. The sisters were already very much secure in His love for them. They already knew that He could heal and do great miracles. But this? This changed everything! However, all of this was not just for the sisters' or Lazarus' benefit. It was also for the benefit of those around them as Scripture tells us, "Many of the Jews therefore, who had come with Mary and had seen what He did, believed in Him" (v.45). It also tells us that "some of them went to the Pharisees and told them what Jesus had done" (v.46). This sets Jesus' own death and resurrection in motion as the Pharisees recognize that Jesus is posing a greater threat to their power and thus, begin to plot His death. So, all that brokenness and pain was also for the benefit of carrying out God's plan to reconcile each one of us to Him and to bring us our peace!

Interestingly enough, the Apostle John makes no mention of the details of Lazarus' illness that caused His death. He makes no mention of Lazarus' reaction to being raised back to life (was it joy or disappointment?). He makes no mention of the aftermath that must have happened in the crowd as a result of this. We don't even read about the sisters' response, and I am sure there was one. Can you even imagine being there in the middle of all of this? Can you imagine the conversations?

Yes, we can be sure there was plenty to talk about. Yet, the only things mentioned here are the new believers and the other witnesses who went to the Pharisees. The focus is not on the crowd. The focus is on Jesus and what He has done, which points the way to the glory and power of the Father, Almighty God displayed in all His majesty at the resurrection of Jesus, Himself. Sweet friend, we can be assured that, just like their tears, not one piece of their brokenness was in vain or wasted, and ours will not be either. Yes, we must mourn. Yes, it hurts. Yes, the pain is ever so real. Yes, sometimes you might feel like it's going to take you out. Yes, all of that is true. But, look up! There is hope! There is always hope if we, like the sisters, believe that we will see His glory, and not only in the last day. Healing is available, and we can experience and celebrate those glimpses of His glory today.

Now, I understand this passage is talking about a physical death. But, are there things that feel dead in our lives today: a dream, a relationship, a marriage, a child gone astray, your family, a career? You fill in the blank. Only you know what "it" is. But you must also know that He is able to bring life back to it. No, I can't promise that it will be just the way you wanted. But this I know: when God shows off and brings something that is dear to our hearts back to life, it is always far beyond our wildest dreams. I can promise you that! Their story is not just kept in the beautiful pages of the Bible; it has jumped out many times into my own life.

> When God shows off and brings something that is dear to our hearts back to life, it is always far beyond our wildest dreams.

And it is ready to jump out into your life, too. I encourage you to take a moment and ponder what is it that He wants to breathe life back into right now, right where you are.

I am fully aware that the distractions robbing us of peace are not always busyness. Some of the things that can rob us of our peace are the circumstances around us that we have absolutely no control over. Some of our brokenness does not come as a consequence of our choosing. However, because our peace is not based on our circumstances but in Jesus, we still have the choice to get back to peace just like the sisters did in the story.

Let's recap what we have read so far in this chapter of choosing peace. The passage in Luke 10 shows us the anxiety that busyness, even good and well-intended busyness, can bring. In contrast to that anxiety is the peace that is found from choosing the good portion, getting to the feet of Jesus. The passage in John 11 gives us a wider window into the lives of the sisters. The John 11 passage was a little more personal, and the distraction is not something they have control over. There is a sense of frustration and maybe even a hint of anger towards Jesus for not preventing the brokenness that came their way when their brother died.

No, their faith had not failed them as they clearly believed that He was able to do something about it. However, they were both distracted by their pain. I think we can all relate here. I know I can. We see their pain. We see their frustration. We see their hope being dimmed by their circumstances. We see that they each mourn in their own way. While they may have felt left behind and uncared for at that moment, it is clear they both end up choosing the better portion. Yes, they do it differently and in their own fearfully and wonderfully made way. Martha responds in her beautiful proactive and pragmatic way. In the midst of her distress, she runs out to meet Jesus while He is still outside the town entrance. Mary in her sorrow would appear to be a little more stuck and maybe needs to mourn the death a little longer. But when Jesus calls for her, she comes out to meet Him, and once again falls at his feet. Yes, we can see that they both feel the brokenness differently. They don't do it very graciously, and one may have more questions than the other. Yet, this passage shows us that they both ended up choosing the good portion! They make their way to Jesus and find peace. In doing so, they are blown away by God giving them a glimpse of His glory right before their eyes.

Wow! Did I already mention that there is so much packed in that passage? There is! No, their faith does not fail them, but it does get shaken and sifted to its core. They become fully aware of their brokenness and the pain it can bring. They wrestled with all of it, and they bring their questions to God who they know loves them and is more than capable to handle their questions. As a result, much like when Jacob wrestled with God in Genesis 32, they are marked and never again the same.

Have you ever been there? In that place that, while you still believed that you would see His goodness and glory, your hope felt a little overshadowed by the pain right in front of you? We all have. At one point or another, we have all asked one or all of the following questions: "Where are you God?" "Why didn't you stop this?" "Why did you let it get to this?" "Don't you care?" "What took you so long?" I know that sometimes it is not easy to admit that we have those questions. As a "good" Christian woman, we are expected to be "just fine" instead of broken, and we are not supposed to question God. I am not suggesting we do either of these. We shouldn't always walk around in gloom with a dark cloud over our heads. There is a difference between embracing our brokenness and having a constant pity party where we complain about life.

I am also not suggesting that we should question God. I would not recommend that at all. However, there is a difference between asking God difficult questions and questioning God. The passage showed us that the sisters didn't question Jesus or His character. Yes, they asked difficult questions, yet they humbled themselves before Him and acknowledged Him being God. Be reminded that Jesus, being God, didn't feel the need to explain Himself or His timing. Yes, He had compassion and felt their pain. He spoke truth into their lives and restored their hope by bringing their focus back to choosing the good portion. However, He didn't feel the need to explain what took Him so long.

I believe it would be good for us to respond in the same way as the sisters responded. But instead, we spend a lot of time and resources asking, "How do I move on and get over this and 'feel' better?" "How do I get away from this brokenness?" I understand the questions and they must be addressed. Life is not always easy. We all have seasons when life's difficulties come our way. I think that Martha and Mary could relate. It wasn't easy for the two sisters we are journeying with. Yet, as difficult as it may have been, they both chose peace.

Okay, time to jump forward to our next passage with the sisters and wrap up our journey with them and how to choose peace. We come full circle in John 12 as we find the sisters back where we first started in Luke 10, opening their home to host Jesus and the disciples. The passage is found in the Gospel of John 12:1–8. I encourage you to look it up and read it.

Yes, we are back at their house, but the scene from Chapter Ten is different. Lazarus, their brother whom Jesus raised from the dead was sitting at the table with Jesus and the disciples. Martha is once again hosting and serving. While Mary is again at the feet of Jesus, it would appear that Martha is not frustrated or distracted. It would appear that she has a new found joy in understanding and using her gift of hospitality to provide rest and nourishment to Jesus and the disciples. The passage does not mention that, but we have learned from our time with sweet Martha that she has no problem communicating her frustrations to Jesus. I like that about Martha. After all, if we have a frustration to share about others, we should share it with Jesus first instead of complaining about it to others. In doing so, He might just show us, as He did with Martha in Luke 10, that we are the ones distracted by many things and in need of choosing the good portion. After all, our own sin is the only sin we can repent from and are held accountable for.

Throughout our journey, we can see that Jesus has a special and unique relationship with them. He was deeply moved by Lazarus' death and the sisters' sorrow in John 11. We see Jesus meets their need in the way they each need Him. He comes back to their home despite the conflict there on previous visits. While the sisters had to wrestle through each of their own conflicts, Jesus has used these conflicts to bring depth, life, and peace to their already strong relationship with Him and with each other. I believe He wants to do the same with the conflicts that come up from our brokenness. He wants to strengthen and deepen our relationship with Him first so that we may in turn encourage one another.

Yes, our sweet friend, Martha was distracted by the busyness that came from her original and genuine desire to serve Jesus by opening her home to Him in the first place. In her *doing* instead of *being*, she was missing the intimacy that comes with sitting at Jesus' feet. Could it be that her frustration with Mary did not come from the work needed in the kitchen as that was expected of them by their culture? Perhaps her frustration came from a hint of envy that she did not have the courage to follow Mary's actions and disregard what others would think of her in going and sitting at His feet. We don't know. What we do know from John 11 is that in her darkest moment and distress, as she is mourning her brother's death, She finds the courage to leave it all behind and runs out to meet Jesus. In her very own way, she chooses to wrestle with the pain and work out her faith. Martha realizes that her choosing does not need to look like anybody else's; she just needs to choose to get to Him. As a result of that transformation, we find her back working in the kitchen, but not because of the expectations

> She finds the courage to leave it all behind and runs out to meet Jesus. In her very own way, she chooses to wrestle with the pain and work out her faith.

of her culture and others. No, she is back in the kitchen serving her Jesus, using her very own gift of hosting to show her devotion, gratitude, and friendship to the One who loved her enough to gently rebuke her, stretch her faith, and give her one of the greatest glimpses of His glory.

We started out with Mary already at the feet of Jesus and getting picked on by her distracted and anxious sister in Luke 10. We will never know on this side of heaven exactly how she got there. But we agree that it no longer matters how she got there. She just did. She chose the better portion. Yes, in chapter eleven we see Mary's deep sorrow of mourning the death of her brother. Yes, she becomes distracted by the brokenness and the pain it can bring. However, she ends up choosing to get back to Jesus' feet, and that portion, her peace, is not taken away from her.

The word *portion* that I keep making reference to here from Luke 10 is often the same word referenced in the Old Testament, indicating close fellowship with God, is to be regarded as one's greatest possession in life. (See Psalm 16:5 and Psalm 27:4.) Or my personal favorite, "My flesh and my heart may fail, but God is the strength of my heart and my portion forever" (Psalm 73:26).

When Mary chose the good portion, fellowship with God, she did not only find peace. Mary also gained a unique ability to discern and understand the heart of Jesus. This kind of deep understanding can only be gained by sitting at His feet, paying close attention to His teaching, and carefully listening to the meaning of every word He was saying. This is best captured when we find her back at His feet here in Luke 12, breaking a jar of alabaster oil. The scene in the house included a dinner honoring Jesus and possibly celebrating the return of Lazarus from the dead. Amidst the celebration there was also, no doubt, some anxiety. The concern, as we read before in John 11:46, had to do with the repercussions of Jesus' miraculous raising of Lazarus from the dead.

The Pharisees were now looking not only for Jesus, but for Lazarus as well. And here they are both sitting at the table with the other disciples.

While they are all aware and concerned and possibly even talking about the situation at hand, Mary is the one who discerns something going on inside the heart of Jesus. She may not know the details of what is coming, but in the uncertainty, she responds and draws closer to Jesus. Once again, she is unconcerned about what others may think of her. She can't help herself. Her intimate study of Jesus reveals something others are missing. Her love and devotion propels her to go and have this beautiful expression of her heart's devotion. She gets back to the feet of Jesus with her oil, and we read that she "anointed the feet of Jesus and wiped his feet with her hair" (v.3). We know this is not just any oil because Judas expresses outrage that she would waste the oil instead of selling and giving the money to the poor. Make no mistake, when we choose to sit at His feet, there will always be someone criticizing the way we do it. Yet, once again because she chooses the good portion, Jesus defends her by saying, "Leave her alone" (John 12:7 NIV).

Everyone wants peace. But not everyone is willing to choose peace even in their most broken moments. Choosing to sit at His feet reveals even the good things that have become a distraction. Being near Him reveals what we need to lay down. Are we ready for the coming change of seasons? Yes, the next Martha season to be actively involved in completing a task or serving in ministry will come; make no mistake about it. There is much to be done for His kingdom. However, our Martha seasons should only come from the overflow of our Mary position.

As we conclude our journey with Martha and Mary in John 12, it would be good to notice something. The atmosphere in the house is different. It appears the sisters recognized that their brokenness is different. How they choose the good portion, peace, is different from others. Their gifts and how they serve with them is different. They no longer compare. They both appear to be at peace even in the uncertainty of knowing there could be a knock at their door from the Pharisees who are looking for Jesus and their brother, Lazarus.

There is, however, something unique to be noted in this last passage. It was Mary's choice to continually find her way to sit in the quiet found only at the feet of Jesus. This sets her apart and brings her in tune with Jesus. Therefore she recognizes what others might be missing. As a result, she gets to prepare His body for His coming death on the cross for our sins, His burial, and His glorious resurrection. And guess what, sweet friend? We can have that same intimacy with Jesus if we make it a point to keep choosing the better portion, peace, by making sure that we are intentional to make time to just sit still before Him, take in the promises found in His Word and know that He is God.

I am forever thankful that I did finally find my way running back to His feet for the unpacking of my boxes. I laid it all down at His feet. The sifting wasn't easy, and I didn't always understand. There are things that even now as I look back I don't understand why some of it had to be the way it was. However, while we don't forget how much it hurt, I no longer focus much on the why *that part* Lord? I have finally come to a place where instead of focusing on the *why* I focus on His faithfulness through it all. I can finally say, "Thank You, Lord…for *all* of it!" Yes, it was difficult. Yes, sifting hurts. But there is no other place I'd rather be than at Your feet. May it all be used to bring glory to Your name."

Sweet friend, I don't know which chapter or season of life you find yourself in. Overwhelmed with the pain of brokenness in your life, I don't know if you are in the kitchen and tired like Martha, or if you're mourning like Mary did when she stared at her brother's lifeless body right in front of her. But this I know: you and I have a Father in heaven who still specializes in resurrecting that

Peace is always available. Peace can be had in the brokenness. But peace must first be *chosen*.

which is dead. Don't let your hope be overshadowed by the tiredness or what may feel very much dead right in front of you. Peace is always available. Peace can be had in the brokenness. But peace must first be *chosen*. Who cares if our choosing looks more like Martha or like Mary, or even a good mix of both. We need to stop comparing. We just need to make a choice. And let me tell you, when we choose the good portion, when we choose to be in close fellowship with our God, when we choose peace, it will not be taken from us. Not now, not in the kitchen, not in a mundane life, not ever!

Remember that I said I had to "unpack my boxes" in order to take my next step with Jesus? Well, just in case your curiosity is like mine, I won't leave you hanging! What was that next step? Well, my sweet friend, you are holding it in your hands. This book was born out of that simple yet profound question my wiser-than-me friend asked me as I unpacked those boxes: "What does peace look like here, Gina?" That was the most difficult question I had to answer in a long time.

But two things I know. One, there is not one single thing that I have laid down that I would trade for getting back to sitting at His feet and drowning in His peace. Two, if any of this brings you the slightest amount of hope and encouragement that peace is readily available to you, or if it gives you even the slightest push to start running back to that position of Mary, I don't say this lightly: it was worth it! Because He *is* worthy, and His kingdom *is* worth it.

Ok. I wasn't expecting the tears that are streaming down my face as I typed that last paragraph of this chapter. And I'm wiping my tears with toilet paper because there are no more tissues in the house at the moment! But here it is. No, it wasn't easy, and it got flat out ugly and really messy at times…but, He is faithful!

Will you choose peace? I hope so. You will never regret that choice.

Exercise

What did you read that stood out to you in this chapter?

What did you learn in this chapter?

Are you currently in a Martha season or a Mary one?

What are you going to do about it?

What does it look like in your life to choose the better portion (Jesus)?

What areas of your life feel dead? Into what areas of our life does God need to breathe new life?

Chapter Four

Journey to Peace

*I*t was the very first snowfall of the year, and I was on my way to visit a friend whose sweet baby boy had just been born. The snow had been coming down since early that morning, and while the roads were very slippery because of how much snow had fallen, I don't think many people minded. Normally, we would already have snow on the ground in this beautiful and often frozen state of Michigan. Besides, there is a rare beauty that most people appreciate when they are able to stop long enough and be captivated by the coziness, especially from inside a warm home, or in this case, a nice, warm car.

As I came to a complete stop for a red light, all of the sudden I noticed a beautiful, small church, the kind you normally see out in the country. To be honest, I didn't just *notice* the church; I was indeed *captivated* by it and the peaceful picture it presented before me.

The sky was bright blue in the back of the crisp, white church with snow perfectly placed on its roof. There was a big, beautiful tree in the front lawn, and the only leaves it held were crystallized ice and powdery snow. And there, between the branches, I noticed my favorite part: the cross. It was a simple, yet beautiful cross at the top of the steeple. The cross was perfectly framed between the crystallized ice and powdery snow branches on the tree with a beautiful, clear blue sky as a backdrop. I realized I only had a short moment before the light would turn green again and I would need to start driving. So, I thought I would take a picture to capture this beautiful moment. That was when, as I rolled down my window to take the picture, a bunch of packed snow from the roof of the car came bursting into my lap, interrupting that peaceful, warm, picture-perfect moment. I frantically opened the door to toss out the snow, only to have even more snow come in (good thing I was at a complete stop, waiting at that red light)!

It was at that moment when I got frustrated and started asking the question, "*Why?* Why does snow have to be so cold and so wet? Why does winter have to come every year? Why can't it just stay warm all year long?" I know, I know, these are all very profound questions. But it was at that moment when God whispered to me, "Gina, yes, snow is wet and cold, and it comes every winter. Yes, winter is a season, and it comes every year. And just like the other seasons, it's not permanent." (Although this is true, sometimes it feels like winter is never going to leave when it bumps a little into spring here in Michigan.)

"You knew it was cold and snowing before you opened the window, Gina. Don't lose sight of what captivated you—my cross in the midst of the wintery snow. Yes, winter is here. Keep your eyes on the cross and adjust so you can be compatible with winter."

Why is it that sometimes it is so difficult to adjust to new seasons? Why is it so difficult to remain at peace when the season changes? I believe the answer is as simple as it is complicated.

I believe it is difficult to remain at peace because we start getting comfortable and think that once we choose peace, we have arrived. Instead of keeping alert for the change in seasons, take the time to slow down long enough to be captivated by that same snow that made me want to scream. Ok, I guess I did scream…out loud!

We somehow get comfortable in the season of our choosing and think that if we could just finally get to feel at peace, life will be just so. Again, we confuse peace with emotion and the season with which we are most comfortable. Yet all throughout the scriptures we are being reminded to take hold of peace.

Now, there are many different versions of the Bible. It's the same Bible, just different translations. All translations stay as close as possible to the original Hebrew and Greek writings. However, because it is difficult to translate word by word from one language to another, some versions may be slightly different in order to provide a better reading flow than others.

While I often read from different versions, for my study time I prefer the English Standard Version (ESV). That is just my personal preference. According to the English Standard Version of the Bible, the word "peace" is mentioned 361 times. That should tell us something. We constantly need to be reminded of peace. In the Gospel of John, chapter 20, we read Jesus saying, "Peace be with you," three times (v. 19, 21, 26). I don't know about you, but that invitation leads me to believe that peace must be chosen in *each* season.

We quickly forget that as long as we are still on this earth, we are on a journey. A journey is the process of traveling to our final destination, and there are many different scenes along the way. Some are stunningly beautiful, and some are not. There can be both sunshine and storms to be found, and there are high points to enjoy the view and mountains that remain to be climbed. We will encounter beautiful creeks to rest upon as well as long rivers to be crossed. We can enjoy grains of sand wiggling through our toes (a personal favorite of mine while sitting at a beach), and we'll also encounter mud to be walked through. Sometimes we can see clear ahead for miles, while at other times we hit a section with thick fog, and we must find our focus point quickly if we want to make it and not get lost in it. We forget that as long as we have not arrived at our final destination, standing in the presence of Almighty God, and we remain in the journey, peace must be chosen daily. We must remind ourselves to do just as Hillsong sings: "Turn your eyes upon Jesus, look full in His wonderful face. And the things of earth will grow strangely dim, in the light of His glory and grace."

> Oh, how very quickly we forget that peace is not the *absence* of conflict and brokenness in our lives but His presence *in the midst* of it all.

Oh, how quickly we forget that because Jesus *is* the One and only true definition of peace; peace *can* be found, and it can be attained, regardless of the circumstances—blessings or trials—that we face on our journey. We quickly forget that the only One who never changes, regardless of where we are in the journey, is Jesus (Hebrews 13:8). Oh, how very quickly we forget that peace is not the *absence* of conflict and brokenness in our lives but His presence *in the midst* of it all.

So now that we have been reminded of the proper definition of peace, knowing full well that peace needs to be chosen daily, let's take a look at where we may end up when we *don't* choose peace along the journey. If we are not careful and depending on our history and life experiences, when brokenness finds us, we may enter into one or all of the following three camps: Camp Blessing, Camp Defeat, and Camp Cynical.

The first camp is the *Camp Blessing*. This is when we get the blessing of enjoying the beautiful parts of the journey, and we get comfortable. We want to stay there forever. We want to live on the mountaintop of the blessing. I think that is really normal. Please, don't feel bad about that. We all long and want to get comfortable and stay in this camp. It makes perfect sense does it not? Why wouldn't we? That is where we were created to live prior to Genesis 3 when sin and brokenness entered the world as Adam and Eve chose the fruit instead of believing and trusting in God.

However, in this Genesis 3 world that we currently live in, mountaintops are not meant to last forever. Mountaintops are there to give us a glimpse of His glory and to remind us that we will make it through the next valley. Yes, we must enjoy every second of the mountaintop and take it all in. But if we don't look at the mountain tops as what they are, glimpses of His glory and a place to catch our breath, when we encounter the

> Mountaintops are not meant to last forever. Mountaintops are there to give us a glimpse of His glory and to remind us that we will make it through the next valley.

next storm, the next mountain to climb, the next river to cross, the next mud to be walked through, and or the next fog to navigate, we will feel as if the rug got pulled from under our feet, and we'll ask ourselves, "What in the world just happened?" If we are not careful, we blame God for what is happening, we blame God for the brokenness, and we can go as far as blaming Him for allowing our peace to be taken away in the midst of the brokenness.

We put up boundaries around our hearts. Sometimes those boundaries turn into walls because of fear to be hurt again. Don't get me wrong. Boundaries are good and a must-have when people hurt us. We absolutely have to. We would be fools if we continually allow for someone to use our hearts to do as they wish. But we also have to be ever so careful. We have to make sure that those boundaries are kept in check before they turn into walls leaving everyone out, including God. The problem with this mentality is that we start treating God as if He is the source of our brokenness, and in our distorted view of Him we end up reducing Him to mankind. We start sounding like Adam in the garden. As he was enjoying the company of that blessing God had given to him in Eve, when the *storm came,* when in His brokenness he needed to give an account, His response was, "It was that women whom You gave me" (Genesis 3:12).

Now, we should not turn this into an "Adam" bashing party. I truly believe that if we are honest and look deep down inside, we do the same thing. I believe that in the midst of our brokenness, in our distress, when the season in the journey changes from blessing to trial, we, too, reduce God to mankind. "It was the (you fill in the blank) blessing that *you* gave me. I didn't even ask for it to begin with. I was just 'fine' without it."

Now, I'll grant you that we may not do it intentionally or that sometimes we may not even be aware we are doing it. But you see, we must be careful that in our vulnerable moments of comfort when the season changes and the *next* thing comes, we are not deceived and become angry with God and therefore put up a boundary with Him. Sweet friend, He is not the One we need to protect our hearts from. He *is* our protector. He is our Creator. He is our Maker, the One who came to rescue us and restore us back to Himself, and in doing so, He brings peace into the mess we created.

Let's move on to the second camp: *Camp Defeat.* This is the camp where instead of getting comfortable in the beautiful parts of the journey, we get stuck in the not-so-wonderful parts of it. We get stuck because we don't want to risk feeling great again, only to end up feeling the pain that comes with *the next* season. We end up stuck because we get tired of the emotional rollercoaster, and so this becomes our comfortable place. How in the world can this be comfortable you ask? Well, I am not sure about you, but through my own journey and conversation with other women, I've realized that often we would rather stay with what we know—even if it's a trial—than risk again.

There is a need for our emotions to level out and settle down, and if we don't allow ourselves to feel great again, if we have no expectations of the blessing, we are not disappointed when the blessing doesn't come the way we dreamed it would come. Or worse yet, in our distorted view of God, we see Him as taking the blessing away…again. We do this instead of recognizing that God never changes, recognizing that we live in a broken world and our broken lives affect and are affected by other broken people. It was just time for the *next* season in the journey. Or as a dear friend of mine often says, "it's just our turn" to walk through the next valley.

Now, I am not sure how often you find yourself in Camp Defeat or what may trigger you wanting to get comfortable and set up your tent here. But I recently learned something about myself. I discovered what may bring me back here, even if for short-lived visits (as well as the times I have been stuck here for longer visits). I'll share an entry from my journal that may explain why this camp has the potential to become a "comfortable" place for me. By the way, Camp Defeat doesn't always look depressing. It may sound and feel depressing, but depending on our personalities, it may not look unappealing. Yes, defeat means that we stop trying. But I think we can be doing great in most areas of our lives and still stop by for visits to the areas parked at Camp Defeat.

I had been wrestling with accepting a blessing God was graciously putting in front of me at the time as He was opening doors that made no sense, except that He was the One opening them. These were doors that made my heart leap a little. Ok, one door in particular that may have even made my heart skip a beat. So what was my problem? I was coming out of a season that felt very much like a long season of learning and coming into a season of surrender. I placed some very much dead and broken dreams at His feet and trusted Him to take care of all it.

However, I had not realized how tired and discouraged my heart had become in the process of picking up the burdens and surrendering them again. I guess my emotions just wanted to settle, and in doing so, my surrendering quickly turned into a "Fine, I will just put it down…again …I'll stop. Maybe I won't ever pick it up again unless You write it in the sky just to make sure."

You see, God had opened doors in that season, and for some reason or another I would not end up being released, free to walk through those doors. Some of those I still don't understand. But understand or not, I finally had come to a place that I could say "*Thank You*! Thank You, Lord for the closed doors." If those doors would have remained open for me to walk through, I would not be sitting here at 3:30 in the morning, typing my little heart out. He used the entirety of that process, plus all the pain and disappointment that came with it, to remind me that not every door He opens is meant to be walked through, but every door He opens is meant to be prayed over so that like Mary, we may choose the better portion. We may choose the door that will keep us on our knees before Him, seeking His kingdom first and trusting Him for the rest.

Now I realize that not every decision holds the magnitude of Y2K consequences or possible "crashes." I honestly believe that if our desire is to serve Him and our motives are pure for His kingdom not ours, He will honor our decisions and graciously redirect us to what He has for us. But then there are those bigger doors, the Y2K moments that require some adapting as they open roads not yet traveled. Doors that become game changers in the journey, like writing a book! Yeah, as much as I love this journey, I am humbled that He would choose to use me. This is so incredibly out of my comfort zone that it is not even funny. God has used this process to stretch me, push me, chase me, and hold me in ways I can't even begin to recount.

Ok, but after all of that, what about that journal entry? I had been diligent in doing all of my research. My man had done research. My man and I had prayed and prayed about it. We prayed together, apart, with others, and we sought out wise council. We examined the contract. Every question we could think of got answered. Everything about this journey has been so far above anything we could have dreamed. No red flags were to be found. So what was holding me back? Here is that journal entry I have been telling you about:

OPEN HEART SURGERY | Hmmm. I think the Lord just revealed something to me. I have realized something new about me in this wrestling process...I think sometimes I may be more scared of the blessing than having to walk through the hard stuff. Not that I think I walk the hard stuff great. I guess I have just been more comfortable with the hard road because I feel like I deserve it. The enemy then takes it a step further and feeds me the lie that not only do I not *deserve* the blessing, I am not *worth* the blessing. Yes, there is some truth to that if I base it on my doings. Yet His truth reminds me that my worth is not based on what good or ugly things I have done. My worth is that I am a child of God (John 1:12). I am His...made in His

> My worth is not based on what good or ugly things I have done.

image (Genesis 1:27). He has chosen me, set me apart for *His* glory, and He dearly loves me (Colossians 3:12). So I will choose Him back along with whatever new or old dreams He has for me. I will walk into all this coming week holds for me with my arms up high and my hands and heart open wide. I will hold nothing back, and I will say, here I am, Lord! If you choose to send me, I will go. I will follow You. I will hold fast to the truth that You are the one who never leaves me nor lets go of me. I surrender *all*. I will seek Your kingdom first and trust You for the rest (Matthew 6:33). Have Your way, Lord! I will *be still* because You are my God, and I am Yours.

What did it mean that I would be still, that He is my God, and that I am His in this season? It meant that after looking at all the different possibilities, doing my research, praying about it, seeking council from His word and my wiser-than-me friends, I only needed to focus on the next obvious step. I needed to stop wondering how it would all work out. I needed to stop allowing my distorted view of God to sneak in on me again, causing me to doubt. Instead, I needed to stop and take the time to reflect on His faithfulness all throughout my life. I needed to trust Him with all of my heart. Because at the end of the day, He is still good and faithful, because He is God.

The third camp we can find ourselves in is *Camp Cynical.* This one is not as easy to identify. I would go as far as to say that, in my humble opinion, it can be the ugliest and most dangerous of all camps. Yes, I can go that far. I can because, while I am not proud of this, the truth is that I have made stops at each one of the camps. Unfortunately, I have not just made quick stops, but I've also been known to set up camp in all of them at one point or another throughout my journey. So why do I think this is the ugliest and most dangerous one? In Camp Blessing or Camp Defeat, it's easier to recognize where we are because there is usually emotion involved. If we catch ourselves, we can make the choice to work our way back to God, back to peace a little sooner. However, when our hearts become so numb to new and old brokenness in our lives, we can check out. We can feel like there is nothing we can do about it, so we go numb instead. We become so numb that sometimes without even knowing it, we have entered and set up camp in this ever-*so*-dangerous campground of cynicism.

Camp Cynical is often the point in the journey in which we lose sight of the bigger picture. We become consumed with the circumstances surrounding us. While fighting our way through the storm to get our hearts back to that peace we all long for, we start wondering if the effort is even worth the struggle. We get comfortable behind our masks, whatever our mask is. Sometimes we don't even recognize the mask we are standing behind, the mask that when someone asks how we are doing, the quick answer is "I'm fine, thanks for asking." And we quickly move on to a different topic. Now, I am not saying that we need to spill our guts out to every person who asks how we are doing. However, when we find ourselves saying "I'm fine" over and over, it's an indication of the location of our heart. When we are running so fast from the brokenness that we don't have the time and space needed to identify what is broken, it gets ugly!

I was recently reminded of this camp as I was looking back through some of the memories of my latest visits here to Camp Cynical. Yes, you guessed it. An old journal entry was found. I was looking for something to use for a project when I came upon it. It was during a time when a lot of brokenness hit all at once: some of my old brokenness, new brokenness, other people's brokenness...you get the idea. Every direction I looked, something kept breaking. It wasn't pretty. It wasn't easy for me to identify the location of my heart because without knowing it, I had landed in Camp Cynical. I had withdrawn from even my closest friends. I didn't do it intentionally, and I am sorry for the hurt I caused some of them. I just knew that I didn't have the space to really let all the pieces hit the ground so that *He* could put them back together.

Let's face it friends, the growing seasons in the journey are difficult. The storms rage; the mountain to climb is steep; the river to cross has currents moving the opposite direction than where we need to go; the mud is thick and ever so messy; and the fog keeps our perspective only to what we can see right in front of us, which often is just more of the same fog.

I will share another piece of my vulnerable heart as I share another journal entry that started my journey back to peace in the midst of the brokenness all around me. It is dated shortly before I experienced the Mary and Martha journey in Chapter Three. This particular night became one of the first "aha" moments for me in that season. I had finally thrown my arms up in surrender earlier that day and said "enough!" I knew I couldn't stay in this camp any longer. My day of surrender came after a sweet encounter in which God allowed for a young woman to catch my heart when in the middle of a communion service, God whispered, "Pray for her." So I did. As I started to pray for her from afar, He said, "Go let her know I love her, I forgive her, I still see her, and I have not forgotten about her."

Oh, Lord, really? It is one of those awkward moments when you doubt yourself because, well, it feels weird to walk up to someone and say, "Ok. I know you don't know me. I know this may sound kind of crazy, because it kind of is. But, I need you to know that I have been praying for you the entire church service, and God wanted me to come and tell you that He loves you, He forgives you, He still sees you, and He has not forgotten about you."

Yep, it is uncomfortable, but I waited for her after service, and that is exactly what I did, word for word. I hate to admit I was still feeling a little awkward until I looked into her eyes and tears were flowing down. For the first time in a while, my mask came off. My cynical heart melted, and I felt alive again. She looked at me and asked, "Who are you? How did you know?" I just smiled and said, "I'm just Gina. God told me!"

Sweet friend, when we embrace our own brokenness, God shows us when others are hurting. We talked for a little while, and she gave me a hug. As she was getting ready to go on her way, she smiled and said, "Thank you! You have no idea the gift God has given me tonight." As I stood there and watched her walk away with her head held high and a smile back on her face, a couple tears fell from my eyes, and I thought to myself, "Oh no, no, no, sweet girl, thank *you*!"

I got home that night and started to type much like I do when He shows off like that. I thank God for three specific conversations I'd had over the course of the prior four weeks because He used them to let me know I had been in the wrong camp for far too long. It was time to start the journey back to peace. Here is a portion of that entry:

Thank You, Lord, for that friend who loved me enough to show up in my driveway and pick me up even after I had texted her that morning and had already told her I was not going to the conference, and she should go without me. But instead, she texted back saying "Get out of bed and get dressed. I am on my way and will be in your driveway soon." Oh, Lord, thank You that she sees past my mask and is willing to hold my hand and drag me out when I am scared to walk through unknown territories.

Thank You, Lord, for that friend that even when I have kept my distance, because she is sensitive to Your Spirit, she could see me drowning behind my smile. She could see the pain behind the mask. So in that moment as I am still walking down the hallway, she sends me a text, "Ok, I won't push you right now. I can see that you are trying hard to press on to what you have going next. You better call me or come see me tonight or tomorrow. If not, I will come find you."

And as you read the text, while circumstances don't change, somehow you find the strength to push through because you can see the light at the end of the tunnel because she noticed, and you can't hide anymore. As scary as that may feel, it's also one of the most freeing moments in the camp.

Thank You, Lord, for that friend who gives me the space to wrestle, but when she sees me sinking and keeps getting my cynical camp answers of "it just is what it is" along with a cynical smile on my face, ready to move on to the next question in the book we are reading together, she loves me enough to risk. She has earned the place in my life to lovingly say, "You know what Gina? I adore you. I know you are hurting, and I will walk this road with you, but you have to do your part. I am no longer interested in your head answers and neither is God. No more! Enough! You are walking a fine line!"

And as the wall around my heart finally starts to fall down, in that moment lies get identified. Tears are wiped as she has me look her in the eyes, and she pours truth into my dried up and numb heart. She reminds me of some of the amazing mountain tops that I've had the blessing to victoriously dance upon. She reminds me of the sand that wiggled through my toes as I was able to finally toss some chains into the ocean and live freely being just me, embracing my brokenness and my God-given calling to be His and for His glory alone. She reminds me of some of the difficult, long, and dry valleys God has carried me through, never forgetting or breaking His promise to "never leave me or forsake me" (Hebrews 13:5). And in that moment, I can finally breathe again freely.

The truth is, I would have left me a long time ago. And then God whispered into my heart, "I know. But I can't do that. I am God, and you are mine. Bring that heart back where it belongs: to me.

Thank You! Thank You, Lord, that not only do You not leave nor forsake your children, You also don't ever let go and are continually coming after me, drawing me back to Yourself. The truth is, I would have left me a long time ago. And then God whispered into my heart, "I know. But I can't do that. I am God, and you are mine. Bring that heart back where it belongs: to me. Stop running from the brokenness all around you. It's time to 'unpack some boxes.' Come with me by yourself to a quiet place and get some rest" (Mark 6:31). Peace can be found in the brokenness because I am there. Trust me. 'Be still, and know that I am God'" (Psalm 46:10).

I share that entry with you because while none of those camps are healthy, like I said before, Camp Cynical can be the ugliest and most dangerous. It can sneak up on us and eat us alive while robbing us of our peace. The roots of Camp Cynical can find a hiding place deep down in our heart. I share that entry with you because, frankly, it's the one that He has chosen for me to share in this camp, not me. It's my least favorite one to share. It feels the most vulnerable to me. However, because of several recent conversations, I've realized Camp Cynical is usually the camp that gets forgotten. It is usually the camp where a lot of us can best hide our brokenness and pretend we are strong by being able to just keep going. We think we are strong because we are able to walk around smiling and say, "I'm fine! You know, it just is what it is!" In Camp Cynical, we walk around as if somehow when brokenness hits our lives and knocks the wind out of us, it will somehow be a negative reflection of God's character, His goodness, or His faithfulness in our lives.

Oh, sweet friend, God is strong enough and big enough and powerful enough to defend Himself. When we walk around wounded, claiming to be healed, that is when people looking into our lives start to wonder if our God is strong enough, big enough, and powerful enough to deliver us. In His Word, God tells us clearly, "My grace is sufficient for you, for my power is made perfect in weakness. Therefore I will boast all the more gladly of my weaknesses, so that the power of Christ may rest upon me" (2 Corinthians 12:9). Here is the best part; when we stop walking around being "just fine" and we realize how desperately we need His grace and His mercy, the sweeter His grace and mercy become.

We have to make the decision to adjust our language from simply, "Yep, it is what it is" to "Yes, it is what it is. Oh, but how I wish it was different, because this hurts! Will you pray for me?" We need to be willing to risk and invest in the kind of friendships that will speak truth and life into our brokenness and not just give us a pat in the back and say, "Yay! Keep going!" These friendships take time to develop and grow. It takes us being willing to invest and risk back in order to cultivate them.

To be honest, I didn't choose any of the relationships I am talking about in my journal entry. And heaven knows if they had known the mess I can be, they would have run the other way and not chosen me either. Each one of those friendships has been as a result of me just being present where God had established for me before the storm hit. But wait! I am getting ahead of myself again. We will talk about how crucial those relationships are in the journey as well as how important it is to keep our motives for relationships in check when we get to Chapter Six. For now, let's get ready to walk the journey to peace.

My prayer and purpose in sharing the different camps with you has been that it would help you identify where you have set up camp, or if you are in a good place, where your default camp might be. We have to be able to identify where we are standing in order to know in what direction we need to move toward peace.

For me, my journey back to peace started during my recent stays in Camp Cynical, when I finally broke down and the tears fell during a conversation with my third friend from my journal entry. That is when I was asked the question that changed everything: "What does peace look like here, Gina?" Why was that such a difficult question? Because she wasn't asking me what peace was. She knew I already knew that. She was asking me what it looked like *here* in the midst of this *brokenness*. But she followed it up with an even more difficult question: "What do you need to do to get to *that* peace?" To be honest, in that moment, I was hoping she would give me the answer. But she didn't. She simply asked the questions, prayed for me, and encouraged me to go back to Scripture. She reminded me to ask the Holy Spirit to reveal the areas of my heart that needed to be looked at. Since peace is His righteousness, He would be the One to give me the answer. As God would show me what peace looked like in that area and what I needed to do to get back to peace, she would ask the same two questions about the next area of my life where brokenness was hitting, and the next one, and the next one. Remember the title of this chapter, "The Journey to Peace"? It is not always a quick fix. It takes time and a willingness to walk the journey.

Ok. Sorry if you have gotten this far in the book, hoping that I had a simple "A-B-C" formula. The journey to peace simply requires a little more effort than that. And hey, if it was a simple formula, I would not be writing this book, and you would not be reading it! But I promise, it will be worth the effort to get back to peace. Our journeys may or may not be similar because we each have our *own*. I can't walk yours, and you can't walk mine. But we can cheer each other on along the way.

I hope and pray that while I can't be sitting next to you right now with a cup of coffee, I pray that you would know that you have everything you need to walk this journey. How do I know? Because you have the Spirit of the living God right there with you. He is available and waiting for you right where you are. My prayer for you has been that this would be a helpful tool to use regardless of what the *next* season holds. I also have been praying that you would invite that friend to walk with you. If you don't have that friend yet, ask God to show you who she is. Maybe start by being that friend to her. And yes, unless it is your husband, that friend needs to remain a *she*. It just works better, and it is safer that way so that feelings and emotions remain in their proper places.

Exercise

I want to invite you to spend time in what has become one of my many favorite passages of scripture: John 15:1–11. I say "has become" because it didn't used to be, and for good reason. Yep, it's the pruning chapter. Ouch! You might be asking, "Gina, what does pruning have to do with peace?" I know. I know. The word peace is not even mentioned in the entire passage once! Hang with me here, though. We are almost to the end of this chapter. Remember, if we've made it this far together, we have agreed already that part of our peace gets lost when we focus on the circumstances around us and when we take our eyes off Jesus. Remember, we agree that we need to be willing to remove the distractions. Like Mary, we need to choose the better portion: Jesus, our peace. We have agreed that peace will be required for us to walk the journey every day so that we can remain in Him, and in doing so, we remain at peace. Well, this is it, and here we are. This is where "the rubber meets the road."

You may want to grab some extra paper and a pen. As you sit down and start reading John 15:1–11, invite the Spirit of the living God to join you and open your eyes to things unseen. Ask Him what things need to be pruned back and what things need to be completely cut and tossed in order to choose peace. Now remember that He won't ask us to cut and toss anything that is established In His Word. So make sure you check the scriptures before you toss anything out.

Before you get started, I want to point out something that is big here. Actually it's huge. Whenever a word or phrase repeats itself in a passage of Scripture, like "Peace be with you" did three times in John 20, it becomes a message that you should pay close attention to. With that in mind, I would like to point out that the word *remain* (or *abide* depending on the Bible version you are reading) shows up eleven times in this passage of eleven verses. That is *huge*! We must *remain* close to Him during this process. The Father is the gardener, and Jesus is the vine who provides life while the gardener prunes and cuts off branches. God is the only One who knows where and what needs to be pruned or cut. Therefore, you must stay close to Him. *Remain* in Him, sweet friend. I say it again, *remain in Him*.

Ok. Find a quiet place and make time for this process. Read the passage slowly a few times, and write down what He brings to mind as you read. Even if you don't have time to do this activity right now, I encourage you to pause reading this book until you can. Don't skip over it! It won't take that long, and it's important not to just skim through in order to check your "box" here.

The Vine and the Branches John 15:1–11 NIV

"I am the true vine, and my Father is the gardener. **2** He cuts off every branch in me that bears no fruit, while every branch that does bear fruit he prunes so that it will be even more fruitful. **3** You are already clean because of the word I have spoken to you. **4** *Remain* in me, as I also *remain* in you. No branch can bear fruit by itself; it must *remain* in the vine. Neither can you bear fruit unless you *remain* in me. **5** "I am the vine; you are the branches. If you *remain* in me and I in you, you will bear much fruit; apart from me you can do nothing. **6** If you do not *remain* in me, you are like a branch that is thrown away and withers; such branches are picked up, thrown into the fire and burned. **7** If you *remain* in me and my words *remain* in you, ask whatever you wish, and it will be done for you. **8** This is to my Father's glory, that you bear much fruit, showing yourselves to be my disciples. **9** "As the Father has loved me, so have I loved you. Now *remain* in my love. **10** If you keep my commands, you will *remain* in my love, just as I have kept my Father's commands and *remain* in his love. **11** I have told you this so that my joy may be in you and that your joy may be complete."

Let's review this passage. What has He revealed to you? It's time to write down the steps you need to take in order to get to your own personal peace. Remember to be patient with yourself. This will take time. It's a process and a journey, but it is worth it.

What did I read?

What did I learn?

What am I going to do about it?

What areas of my life am I being distracted by and what areas need to be pruned?

What areas of my life need to be cut and tossed so that I may be able to get back to that position of Mary and choose the better portion, Peace?

I have read this passage several times. However, I can remember three specific times that I have walked in depth through this passage in my walk with Jesus. During each of those three encounters, He has revealed to me something new that has transformed my heart. The message never changes, but I love it when the Spirit of the living God reveals to me something I hadn't seen before. Each time I have been brought closer to Him. Each time, while not always fully understanding, at the end of the pruning and cutting of branches, I have been able to say, "Thank You Lord for the pruning and the cutting of the branches that got in the way of me *remaining* in you. Yes, it hurt. Yes, it was hard. Yes, it was messy. But thank You, Lord. Thank You for all of it. Thank You that life is growing again in areas that had felt numb and dead for a while." Sweet friend, I believe that is when peace is truly found, when we are able to say "Thank You, Lord for all of it." Not "Thank You for the brokenness." But "Thank You that Your peace is still found in the midst of it."

Until we arrive at our final destination and no longer walk this earth, remember that the journey continues, so keep walking. Put one foot in front of the other. Don't worry about what is next or even concern yourself when it will come. We know that seasons change, and the next season *will* come. The beautiful thing is God is already there. If we keep remaining in Him, if we keep choosing Him, we will continue to remain at peace in the midst of whatever brokenness the next season might bring.

My prayer for you as we end this chapter together is this: "I pray that God, the source of hope, will fill you completely with joy and peace because you trust in him. Then you will overflow with confident hope through the power of the Holy Spirit" (Romans 15:13 NLT).

Chapter Five

Holding On To Peace

So here we are, sweet friend, the chapter in which we will be encouraged and learn how we can practice holding on to peace, regardless of the season we find ourselves in this journey.

Before we start, I believe it's important for us to review a little bit and be reminded of what we have covered thus far. Chapter One presented the biblical definition of peace as God's righteousness displayed in Jesus. Chapter Two was our crash course of Genesis 1–3 covering *who* it is that we were created to be, where we learned what is broken in the world as well as what is broken in our very own lives. And we learned the importance of *why* that brokenness exists. In Chapter Three we explored the lives of our dear friends Martha and Mary. We learned that the better portion, Jesus, and our peace, must be chosen in the midst of life happenings, serving, distractions, uncertainty, and pain. In Chapter Four, we were reminded that because of the brokenness of

Genesis 3, until Jesus comes back to turn this upside down, broken world right side up, we will find ourselves in a journey in which peace will need to be continually chosen. We learned about Camp Blessing, Camp Defeat, and Camp Cynical. We learned that regardless of what camp we are prone to camp in, we can always find our way back to peace. Through it all, we have learned that peace is not the absence of conflict or brokenness in our lives, but Jesus' presence in the midst of it.

Remember the journal entry in which I mention a conference I tried to cancel going to, but my friend told me to get out of bed because she would be in my driveway soon? Well, I am so glad I went. I just wish I had not worn mascara that day. There I was, sitting in the middle of a large auditorium with tears flowing, ok, gushing, out of my eyes. The speaker was teaching about Old Testament Joseph and the dream he had been given early in his life. But he walked a long and difficult road before that dream was realized.

Sandwiched between Genesis 37 and Genesis 50, Joseph goes from being the favorite to enduring the pain of losing his family through his brothers' betrayal when they threw him into a pit and then sold him into slavery. He endured the false accusations of Potiphar's wife and spent many nights in prison. I don't think Joseph ever envisioned that's where the journey to his dream would take him. Yet when we read Joseph's story, we don't find him complaining. Through it all, we read about his unwavering dependence and trust in God.

Joseph remained steadfast through the heartache and disappointment, and while he experienced discouragement, he never lost sight of his dream. As a result, even though Joseph no longer held the "favorite one" status his brothers accused him of, it is clear that God's favor remained with him through it all; God continued to use him in the process, in the waiting.

So what had me in tears at the conference? The conviction of the Holy Spirit as He gently whispered, "Why did you let go of my dreams for you?" I normally would have quickly given Him my list of excuses. And man, I had some really good excuses; some of them may have even been valid ones. But I couldn't. Not this time. Not after being reminded of Joseph's story and his unwavering trust. Truth is I couldn't do much at the moment other than just breathe as tears were filling up my eyes.

My wiser-than-me friend, who would not let me stay in bed that morning and who has walked a few steps ahead of me in life, reached out and gently grabbed my hand and said, "You are going to be okay. Let them fall." And that I did. Although, I am not sure I had much of a choice. But at least this time I wasn't fighting to push them back like I had done before, walking up and down the aisles in the middle of a store looking for a dressing room. No, here I was, in the middle of an auditorium full of strangers, letting my tears roll down my face, taking quiet, deep breaths in and out, no longer running from the pain or wishing it to go away. For the first time in a long while, I didn't want to be numb from the pain and disappointment that had come my way. Yes, life had taken some unexpected turns, affecting everything I held dear to my heart. But at that moment, I no longer cared. There I sat, mascara running along with the tears and all.

Yes, Joseph experienced a change of plans, and I am sure his dream was not unfolding the way he thought God would do it; of that I am sure. However, we don't know much about what Joseph thought of his circumstances and his journey, or if he may have felt that the dream he had been given was fading away. We don't know, because we don't read about Joseph complaining, letting go or forgetting the dream he had been given. I wish the same could be said of me, but unlike Joseph, when the unexpected turns started to come my way, I don't think it could be said that I didn't have my share of complaining to God and asking Him a few questions.

Yes, I had questions, actually many of them. But they can be summed up with this, "So, I finally said yes to the dreams you gave me all those years ago; I finally jumped in with both feet, and now you change the plan? Where are You in all of this, God?" Yeah, that was not very peaceful of me. Martha showed us in Chapter Three that God is more than capable to handle our big and difficult questions. But we must also remember to *Whom* we are talking. The story of Martha and Mary reminds us that while He is compassionate and feels the pain of our grieving, He does not feel the need to explain Himself to us. We quickly forget that He is God, and we are not. We quickly forget that while we may have some really great plans for His kingdom and often with the right motives, He has the better plan because He is God, and we are not.

When I finally stopped long enough to hear what I was actually saying, I felt the guilt and shame that came with it. After all that God had saved me from, after all the times I had drowned in His faithfulness and mercy throughout my life, who was I to ask these questions of Him? However, I don't believe my questions are what broke God's heart. I believe what broke God's heart was my tragic mistake of trading His truth for a lie. I didn't give Him my guilt and my shame. I didn't choose Him, the better portion. I didn't *choose peace*. I didn't choose the truth that He always loves me and will never leave me. I gave up on His dreams for me. Instead of reaching out to the people who I knew loved me and would "walk the mess" with me, I decided to let the guilt and the shame of not trusting God find a place in my heart to rest, much like when I was nine years old and my dad died. But rest is *not* what I found, let alone peace.

Unlike Joseph, I allowed the unexpected turns in my life to set God's dreams for me aside. I traded being still before Him for the restlessness that comes from striving to please others. In the process of it all, I landed in the identity crisis I had been wrestling through. In the midst of that identity crisis, the dreams He had given me started to fade away. As I held tight to the lie, the dream didn't just keep fading away, I eventually laid it completely down and walked away from it.

As I kept holding tight to the lie, more brokenness came my way that I had no control over. That is when I eventually found my way to Camp Cynical. I kept striving until the "boxes" in my heart started bursting open. God put a specific search and rescue team together with His faithful servants. The same faithful friends I had been trying to keep my distance from were the ones who reminded me that pushing away and trading in my brokenness was not going to work any longer. They reminded me of the dreams God had given me and that if I was going to pick up that dream He had for me again, then it was time to start answering my wiser-than-me friend's questions of what peace looked like in each "box" as it burst open. What was I going to do in order to find my way back to peace? There was no way around it; I was very aware of the boxes in my heart, much like the boxes in my basement storage which were finally being unpacked. It was time to get things back in order so I could start working my way back to my God-given calling.

What is my God-given calling? The same one you have: to be His, for His glory alone, no matter the season of my life, and to be just like Joseph who remained who God had said he was. As a result, God was able to use Joseph regardless of Joseph's location, position, or circumstances. Joseph remained being God's, for His glory, by trusting Him and waiting on His timing to fulfill His dreams for Joseph.

> When we trade in our *just being* for *striving*, we become slaves to expectations.

When we trade in our *just being* for *striving*, we become slaves to expectations. When those expectations, good or not so great, are not met, we become prisoners. In this process we lose sight of the dreams God has given us, and we forget *Whose* we are, and therefore, we forget *who* we are. In the midst of our brokenness, we become restless and anxious—the complete opposite of peace.

Yes, Joseph experienced way more hardship and unexpected turns in the journey to His God-given dream than I have. Yet, he never stopped being who God created him to be. Joseph must have come to the realization that maybe the entire journey was part of God's dream for him (the journey, not the brokenness caused by others). What makes me think that? Like all of us, Joseph had many lessons to learn in the process; he needed to be equipped spiritually for the weight of the responsibility that would come with the dream. Joseph used His God-given gift no matter what his physical location was. Joseph kept interpreting dreams that others couldn't understand.

Yes, God used the tragedies and disappointments in Joseph's life to prepare him for the dream that God had given Him. Joseph had to learn the humility required to respond with compassion when the dream came to be, the type of compassion and humility required for Joseph to be able to say to his brothers, "'Do not be afraid. Am I in the place of God? You intended to harm me, but God intended it for good to accomplish what is now being done, the saving of many lives. So then, don't be afraid. I will provide for you and your children.' And he reassured them and spoke kindly to them" (Genesis 50:19–21 NIV). Joseph could have responded differently to his brothers, and many of us would have understood that different reaction. But Joseph doesn't do that, because he can't. In the midst of all the brokenness of the journey, Joseph kept his heart close to God's instead of digging and belly flopping into His own pity party.

Sweet friend, I don't know about you, but it has been my experience that if I get as much as the smallest grin on my face when I hear of someone who has intentionally (or not) hurt me struggling, I better catch myself and listen to the whisper of God's Word that, "But by the grace of God I am what I am, and His grace to me was not without effect" (1 Corinthians 15:10). Because when we experience the fullness of God's grace (His unmerited favor), we are drawn into the sweetness of His mercy (His unmerited compassion). And in doing so, humility draws us to our knees. It is in those moments that we best display the image of the One we were created to reflect. His love, joy, *peace*, patience, kindness, goodness, faithfulness, gentleness, self-control are best displayed in us when we stand in our true identity, in the truth of who God says we are: *His*! When we do that, when we stand in our identity of the God who created us, we don't take the slightest pleasure in seeing others hurting.

It is only when we stand in our true identity as children of Almighty God that our peace is restored, and we can say, "It is well with my soul, it is *all* well with my soul." Then we are able to forgive because we are no longer concerned about others getting away with the injustice or the brokenness. While we may never fully understand some of the unexpected turns in our lives, we can trust that God doesn't waste one tear that fills up or falls from our eyes. And in that moment, our hearts are set free. We don't push back the tears or worry about mascara running down our face. In that moment, we are able to sit with a friend in the middle of a large auditorium while she just sits next to us, quietly praying for us as each tear falls.

> He knows that in our brokenness, we will never measure up to His standard, so He made a way back to the Father, a way for us to be able to choose peace in the brokenness.

Instead of needing to find a dressing room to belly flop into our pit, our heart is now running back to Jesus. He knows that in our brokenness, we will never measure up to His standard, so He made a way back to the Father, a way for us to be able to choose peace in the brokenness.

We must agree that we are not all broken in the same ways and that not every part of our lives is broken. Each of us has only walked our own journey, and therefore, our brokenness, our stories, and experiences and how they affect us are unique. I hope you understand that. However, in my study and understanding of Scripture, I have come to believe with everything in me that the root is our identity issue. If not kept in check, it can quickly move from an issue to an identity crisis, like the one I had landed in which allowed for the brokenness in the "boxes" of my heart to become my identity.

Now, I can only speak for myself here. But before I do, I must give a full disclosure. One of my greatest joys in life has been the blessing and honor to be my fearfully and wonderfully made man's wife and the mom of our sweet (most of the time) and fearfully and wonderfully made children. If I am not careful, those roles and those gifts can become my identity. As fearfully and wonderfully made as they each are, they too are broken beings living in this broken Genesis 3 world.

I love my man and each of our kids with a love that I can't find words to describe. Yet as much as I love them, as much joy as they bring to my life, and as blessed as I count myself for these gifts God has graciously given me, I hope you notice that I have mentioned *they are broken, too*. We all are. Our family has not been spared from brokenness and the pain it brings. However, we have also experienced and shared the peace that comes when in the midst of it, we hold on with all we have to the hand of God and to each other.

I don't know what you would consider to be that special part of your joy or blessings you hold dear and near to your heart. I say "part" because only Jesus can be our complete Joy. I don't know what your dreams for His kingdom are, or the gifts He has equipped you with to carry those dreams out. But I am sure you have them. I can only share what my dreams are, according to what He has revealed to me.

I will zoom into that calling to "be His, for His glory alone." We put so much mystery in that word "calling," don't we? I agree that we all have different gifts and passions. I get it. I am passionate about encouraging women to take their next step in their journey with Jesus, I truly am. Living out my calling causes butterflies to take permanent residence in my heart. God ignites that passion, that dream He has given me, through the privilege of teaching and sharing what I have learned in His Word. Okay, our gifting may not look the same, but that calling? That calling has been given to *all* of us in the same way, "And Jesus came up and spoke to them, saying, 'All authority has been given to Me in heaven and on earth. Go therefore and make disciples of all the nations, baptizing them in the name of the Father and the Son and the Holy Spirit, teaching them to observe all that I commanded you; and lo, I am with you always, even to the end of the age'"(Matthew 28:18–20). That is it! No mystery on what the calling is.

My favorite part of that scripture is the promise that comes with it at the end of verse 20: "I am with you always, to the end of the age." If we have learned nothing else, we have learned that if He is always with us, peace can *always* be found, chosen, and had. Jesus is always there waiting for us to *show up*, so He can *show off*, and His kingdom can move forward.

In order for us to hold on to peace, whether in the brokenness or in our well-intended good doings for God, we must model what Jesus did in John 6 after He performed many miracles and the crowds were following Him. After Jesus fed the five thousand, the people wanted to keep Jesus near so He could keep performing miracles (John 6:14–15). But we read that Jesus withdrew to a mountain instead. They wanted to keep Jesus around again after He walked on water. They wanted Jesus to stay but not for the right reasons (John 6:26). Jesus wraps up John 6 by saying that He has *not* come from heaven to do the will of the people; He has come to do the will of the Father (John 6:38).

Sweet friend, here is what I have learned after many failures: if and when that storm comes, we allow the busyness and demands of life to keep us from staying close to His word and to His heart, we quickly forget that no one has the authority to define us or us them. So in order to keep our peace, we must stay close to His word. It has to be more than memorizing passages to simply increase our knowledge. It has to be more than giving "cookie cutter" answers to our Bible study questions. By the way, I highly recommend staying close to His word and memorizing scripture, but we intentionally need to make time in our lives to "Be still, and know that He is God" (Psalm 46:10), to humbly come before Him and say, "Search me, O God, and know my heart; test me and know my anxious thoughts. Point out anything in me that offends you, and lead me along the path of everlasting life" (Psalm 139:23–24 NLT).

> We must allow His word to soak into our hearts and reach the depths of our souls. We must let the knowledge stored up In our heads find Its way to our hearts.

We must allow His word to soak into our hearts and reach the depths of our souls. We must let the knowledge stored up in our heads find its way to our hearts. When we do that, we understand who He says that *we* are, and we can identify the lies we are fighting.

So how do we do it, and who in the world has that kind of time, right? Okay, here we go. Here is what I have learned. Just like Jesus, in order to carry out the will of the Father, we must only listen to the Words of the Father. And that requires discipline. I know, I know, this is coming from a fly-by-the-seat-of-my-pants, free spirited girl. Hey! All the more reason discipline is needed! I'll be honest, while discipline has not always come easy for me, I crave discipline. I know, it sounds confusing; however, I have learned to love discipline and appreciate it as it shows me where the lines are. There is a rare *freedom* in knowing where the lines are and that I can chose which side of the boundaries I play in. I can either be safe or take a chance. So, is discipline worth it to stay close to our Heavenly Father and remain at peace? Yes!

It was at that conference with my mascara and all my makeup finally gone, that I was reminded of an exercise, a tool that God used to bring healing to my heart as I first embarked in the journey of finding peace in the brokenness all those years ago when I first gave my life to Jesus. Think of your life as surrounded by radio stations. Depending on our history and life experience we will tune in to whatever radio station plays the music with which we are most familiar and comfortable. We may not necessarily enjoy all the music that station plays, but we often stay there because it's what we know. And like we talked about in Chapter Four, there is comfort in familiarity. But the longer those songs and their words play in our minds, the more they start taking residence in our heart. We start believing the lyrics, holding tight to them and belly flopping into our pits.

In order to hold on to peace, we have to remain close to Jesus by being willing to prune the distractions. (Remember our exercise from Chapter Four?) We must get back to the Father and listen to His Word so that we may know His will for us. We must get back to the Father in order to be restored to Him and find peace, the kind of everlasting peace we will be able to share with others. In order for us to keep hearing the words of the Father, it will require us to dig in a bit deeper and do some homework.

> In order to hold on to peace, we have to remain close to Jesus by being willing to prune the distractions.

Just like you, I have responsibilities that can quickly fill my schedule. As a result, I've had to set up rhythms in my life that allow me the space and discipline to use this tool about every three months or so. I keep my notes handy to keep my heart in check in between times of doing this exercise. No, it doesn't mean I let go of my responsibilities in the process, it simply means it has become a priority in my life. Sometimes this means I sacrifice sleep either in the morning or at night. (I am more of a night owl and always felt guilty for not being a morning person. So I am here to say this: God is available *around the clock*. No guilt! Just get it done, ok?)

When I don't make this a priority, my peace can slowly start to fade away. Like I've said before, I don't breathe very well without staying in His word. I quickly tune in to my old radio stations and make up the words to my own songs, or I tune into someone else's station and start listening to the words of their songs.

I don't know what the words are in the songs that play on your radio station or who wrote them. They can be words like "fear," "pride," "failure," "not enough," "neglect," "abandonment," "loneliness," or "abuse." Again, you are the only one who can fill in the blank. *You know your own words.* Chances are that if you stop for a second, you would quickly hear them. But I don't want you to stop there just yet. I want you to identify them, write it down on the side of this page and keep moving along. We will come back to them in a few moments as we do the exercise and look at a passage of Scripture that will help us remain at peace longer in the brokenness and help keep our restless times in between shorter.

Before we move on to our homework at the close of this chapter, I want to share a quick story that happened here at the farm recently. We call our home "the farm" because, while we've had a family dog for years, our family has added two gecko lizards, a guinea pig, and nineteen chickens to this home where we plan to live a long time. I know, and if that wasn't enough, the kids are currently praying for a cow, a goat, and a turtle. I am just praying that God will answer their prayers in my (and my man's) favor!

So last week was a difficult one around the farm. It was the first time we lost chickens to a predator. While we all love the chickens, we are all very much aware that they are Caleb's, our oldest son's, chickens. He is the one who, since day one, goes out every morning before school and feeds them. Then he goes back out when school is done and checks on them. During the summer, he would take a beach chair out to the coop to read (Caleb reads *all* the time), and before we knew it, the chickens would be all around him. We even started calling him "the chicken whisperer."

So knowing all of that about our Caleb, you can see how he would be the one who would take it the hardest when we lost so many chickens. I desperately pleaded with God to give me the words as I braced myself and shared the news with him. It was difficult, but Caleb responded well to the news. We even talked about what we could do to better protect the rest of the chickens from predators.

With a sigh of relief at his response, I went on about my day. We all did actually. Well, all except Caleb. As I looked out the window, I could see him walking the woods and looking under bushes. I have to be honest, I didn't think much would come of it, but I figure I'd just let him do it in the hope that it would help him with the mourning process. But as I was standing in the kitchen getting ready to start dinner, Caleb come running in from the back door, "MOM! MOM! MOM! Where are you?"

So I quickly ran back to him, and as I turned the corner, he stood there with a big smile on his face. With a chicken in his arms, he said, "I found Gretchen! She is wounded and lost a lot of her feathers, but she is alive!" I celebrated with him and then watched him hold Gretchen, the chicken, close to his heart as he walked out back to the coop where he gently put her down.

And guess what? He still didn't come inside; he went back to the woods looking again, and he found another chicken. Two chickens had survived the predator attack. She was wounded just like the other chicken. She had lost feathers but was alive and could recover. And just like the time before, he swept her into his arms, held her close to his heart, and walked her back to the coop where he gently put her down, too. He wouldn't come back in the house until he had walked the woods and looked under every bush. He had to know that there were no more chickens left out there.

As I stood by the window watching my son take care of his chickens, tears started rolling down my face. I was reminded that *that is what God does with us*. Even when people have moved on and have gone about with their lives and the brokenness remains, Jesus never does. He never just moves on. He continually goes out into the woods, looking under every bush for the lost and the wounded. "He tends his flock like a shepherd: He gathers the lambs in his arms and carries them close to his heart" (Psalm 40:11 NIV).

Sweet friend, I don't know where you find yourself in this process of *peace in the brokenness*. I don't know if you are still out there in the woods like our lost and hurting chickens were. I don't know if you are under a bush taking shelter, trying to catch your breath. I don't know what wounds your heart holds or how many feathers you have lost. But this I do know: our Heavenly Father sent the good Shepherd, Jesus, to bring us peace. He is looking for you, ready to gather you up in His arms and carry you close to His heart. He is ready to mend whatever brokenness, big or small, you find yourself in. And I know this, no matter where you find yourself, if you want to hold on to peace, you have to get back to the Father through Jesus, the good Shepherd. My prayer is that you will let Him carry you. By doing so, you will be able to hold on to peace longer, and your restlessness from the brokenness that remains will be shorter.

Exercise

Be sure you have extra paper, a Bible, and a pen handy.

Are you ready to dig in deeper? Great! Saddle up, my sweet friend! I promise it will be worth it!

Keep in mind that this should not become an emotionless ritual. It's an exercise to keep your heart open to the Father and your identity and peace in place. In my prayers, sometimes all my heart can cry out is, "Help!" This is the example that Jesus left for us when He said:

> "Pray, then, in this way: Our Father who is in heaven, Hallowed be Your name. Your kingdom come. Your will be done, on earth as it is in heaven. Give us this day our daily bread. And forgive us our debts, as we also have forgiven our debtors. And do not lead us into temptation, but deliver us from evil. [For Yours is the kingdom and the power and the glory forever. Amen.]" Matthew 6:9–14 (NASB).

It always amazes, but no longer surprises me, that when we feel most broken, we often long to be heard; we talk to someone, a friend, a parent, a spouse, our dog, *anyone* who will listen! Yet, all the while, we often bypass the One who is always available and who sent His Son to make a way for us to bring our heart to Him. My hope is that if we understand prayer to be what it is—*communication with the Father*—we will begin to grasp the beauty of it and the peace it makes available as we remain connected to the Father.

Finding Our Way Back To The Father

1. Our Father who is in heaven, Hallowed be Your name

While we come to the Father through Jesus, Our request is directed to the Father. Our prayer addresses the Father, our maker, and our identity giver. He is the Creator of it all and to whom all things are possible. This is important because it requires that we acknowledge what we know and believe about His character. The word *hallowed* is making reference to His holiness, which is to be revered. As we call on our Father whose name is holy, we can't help but acknowledge what is needed and required on our end: our humility and our worship.

What words communicate who you believe God is?

What words would you use to explain His character? (Psalm 119:68, 1 John 4:7–10, Galatians 5:22–23)

What lies do you believe about God?

What "radio stations" are you listening to that cause you to have a distorted view of who God is? What keeps you from coming to Him as your Father?

What *box labels* have you allowed to be your identity?

Based on who God says you are in the scriptures, created in His image
(Genesis 1:27) what words does He use to describe you? (John 1:12,
Colossians 3:12–17)

What steps do you need to take to remove the lie, replace it with His
truth, and gain peace?

2. Your kingdom come

This part addresses our need to remember that it is all about His kingdom
and our commitment to it. Nothing else will last. It is important to
know that the Kingdom of God we are referring to is anywhere and
everywhere that Jesus reigns. As followers of Christ, we are making the
proclamation that Christ reigns in our hearts and over our lives as King.
If that is our claim, the Kingdom of God is all around us, and we should
continually do our part in the advancement of his Kingdom. We have a
responsibility to live lives that are reflective of His love and obedient to
His Word. We must live lives that reflect our commitment and desire to
honor Him in the midst of our brokenness. It is in those moments that
His strength is best displayed in our weakness. It is in those moments
that His image is best displayed in us.

• Is my life one that reflects Jesus and the righteousness of God?
  (Philippians 4:8)

- Is He King, ruling over my life? (Psalm 19:14)

- What keeps me from giving God reign over *all* of my heart?

- What active steps of obedience do I need to take so He has all of me?

- How do I replace the lies with His truth so that He reigns? (2 Corinthians 10:5, 2 Corinthians 5:17)

- What is my part in the advancement of His kingdom all around me? (Matthew 28:19–20)

3. Your will be done, on earth as it is in heaven

This might be one of the most difficult parts of our prayers. Here, after wrestling with God, we acknowledge that we don't have to always understand, but because we have replaced the lies we believed about His character with His truth, we *can* trust Him. Because we trust Him, we can say, "Yes, Lord! Have Your way." This allows us to submit to the will of the Father. How do we know His will? His will is always revealed to us in Scripture. There are no areas that He has left out for our own "revelation." If anyone ever suggests something different from what Scripture teaches, run from it! In all we seek to do, we must always take into account "the whole council of God" (Acts 20:27–30). God's will never contradicts His Word.

- What areas of my brokenness need to be surrendered to the Father?

- What does it mean for me to trust Him to work things out for *my* good and *His* Glory? (Romans 8:28)

- What active steps of obedience do I need to take in order to trust that His plans for me are good, even when I don't understand, so I surrender to His will? (Jeremiah 29:13, 12, 11—read them in that order)

4. Give us this day our daily bread

This is the acknowledgement of our dependence on Him and our trust in His provision. He provides for all our needs. I realize that Scripture here says *daily bread*, which is talking about our physical needs. It is my personal opinion that, while the literal reading of this is in reference to the food that sustains our physical bodies, I believe we can ask Him for *whatever* the need is to sustain us and carry us throughout our day. I believe that if we are asking Him for provision according to His will, He will provide it. Again, it may not look like what we think it should; however, if we take the time to look at our lives and within ourselves, we would see His provision in our physical, emotional, and spiritual needs.

- What are my "daily bread needs" to sustain me and keep me at peace in the midst of brokenness?

- What lies have I believed that keep me from asking God for His provision? (Romans 8:32, 1 John 3:22, John 15:16)

- What active steps of obedience do I need to take to trust His provision in every area of my life? (Matthew 6:33)

5. Forgive us our debts, as we also have forgiven our debtors.

Our prayer to *forgive us our debts* is not one for salvation. A child of God does not need to ask daily for salvation. Our salvation is secure the moment we acknowledge our sin and our need for our Savior, Jesus, to help restore us with the Father. This prayer is for restoration because the brokenness of our sin hinders our daily relationship and interaction with the Father. As we receive His forgiveness, it should move us to forgive others, too. Having the proper understanding of forgiveness is huge here. I don't know about you, but the reason I used to have a difficult time with this part of the Lord's Prayer was because I thought that my *debtor* was getting away with the *debt*. However, it doesn't mean that at all. Forgiving others allows us to get out of the way and trust God with the outcome. But we should put healthy boundaries in place so that others don't continue to hurt us. This frees our hearts to be in daily fellowship with our God, not distracted by the injustice of what others are doing, but trusting God to take care of the injustice.

- What areas of my brokenness and sin are hindering my daily interaction and fellowship with the Father?

- What debts do I need to forgive? (Matthew 6: 14–15)

- Is there any forgiveness that I am willingly withholding from others? (Matthew 5:7)

- What active steps of obedience do I need to take in order for my debts to be forgiven by God and for my fellowship with Him to be restored?

6. And do not lead us into temptation, but deliver us from evil

While God himself will not tempt us, He does *allow* situations to come our way in which we will be tested. Will we choose sin or will we choose Him? That is exactly what happened in Genesis 3 with Adam and Eve. He allowed the temptation to come. He allowed them to choose their will or His. I often wonder what would have been if Adam and Eve had taken the time to call upon God in their time of temptation. How would life be different if they had just taken the time to ask God for help? We must be mindful that we have an enemy who is constantly seeking to destroy us (John 10:10), and we must believe the Father is the One who has the power to deliver us through Jesus. It only makes sense that we would ask for His deliverance from the enemy of our souls: Satan.

- What areas of my life am I more vulnerable to fall into temptation, especially in the brokenness?

- What keeps me from asking God for help and deliverance when temptation comes my way?

- What steps of obedience do I need to take so that, in my brokenness, I may run to the Father for deliverance in time of need? (Psalm 50:15, 2 Samuel 22:1–4, Hebrews 4:15–16)

7. [For Yours is the kingdom and the power and the glory forever. Amen.]

While these words are not included in all Bible versions (they are not found in the early manuscripts), there is no theological flaw in the words themselves. Therefore, we can take liberty in studying them. It is appropriate for us to include them in our prayers as they bring us back full circle from where we started. First, we acknowledge the Father, His authority, and our commitment to the advancement of His kingdom. So we start and finish our prayer acknowledging the Father, being about His kingdom and Him being worthy of our worship.

Take the time to respond to the Father now. Write your prayer in as if you are writing Him a letter. Be vulnerable with Him. Remember, He is your Creator, the Father who loves you so much that He sent His only Son to restore your relationship with Him and bring you His peace in the midst of the brokenness. Close your letter to Him by answering the following question: *What will my act of worship look like in this next season?* Keep this handy as a point of reference when you feel yourself moving away from peace. Yes, this requires time, discipline, and effort. Remember what my grandpa used to say? "Anything worth having will require work and effort." I can't think of anything more worthy of time and effort than to get back to finding, choosing, and staying at peace in the brokenness.

Exercise

My response to God:

My *act* of worship to God in this next season is:

Chapter Six

The Brokenness That Remains

As I sat down to write this final chapter, I found myself thinking the same thing I have thought each time since Chapter One: "This is going to be the most difficult chapter to write." And at the conclusion of each chapter I have said the same thing: "Yes, that was indeed the most difficult one...yet."

What makes it difficult? While we can find peace with our past brokenness and the healing God provides for us in Jesus, until Jesus returns, there will be some *brokenness that remains*. Although we finally understand the *why* of the brokenness (Genesis 3) and that peace is not dependent upon our circumstances, we still have to walk through and deal with the brokenness that remains. And while we understand that God is the only One we need in order to be at peace, we still live in this Genesis 3 world where brokenness resides. We can't just walk away from the lingering brokenness; we can't just keep shoving it under the rug thinking it has no effect on our lives; we can't just keep ignoring it and hoping it will disappear before Jesus returns to remove all of the remaining brokenness. But we are also not supposed to keep getting stuck in it. Jesus, the better portion we learned about in Chapter Three, must be chosen over the brokenness that remains.

Let me share an example of what I mean. My man and I had a very lively discussion recently. We were both tired and became frustrated over something really dumb. Are you ready for it? We were arguing over three screws in a wall. Yep, I know, pathetic at its best. I will spare you the details of the lively conversation. I do, however, need to give you a little bit of background about the situation and why those three screws on the wall got the best of us.

Remember the dream home we purchased four years ago? The one we lovingly call "The Farm" and where, little by little, we get glimpses of God's mercy and faithfulness? Yeah, well the reason we were able to buy this dream home in our dream location is because it had some work to be done and some love to be given to it. It was mostly cosmetic work until we had to replace 26 windows immediately if we wanted to stay warm through the winter in this lovely state of Michigan. (And 26 windows was only about half of the total number of windows that needed replacement in the house.) That first winter, we also had some broken pipes, among other minor but important things here and there, that quickly drained the cosmetic budget.

Please don't misunderstand me. We love our home, and we thank God for it on a regular basis. Yes, we love this home even with all the *broken* things that remain to be fixed. We still believe it is everything we dreamed of when we walked through it for the first time four years ago. Yes, I have even learned to look past the old, original linoleum floor in our kitchen (which is finally and officially in the process of being replaced). Even when our home feels more like a "blood, sweat, and tears home" because of the *brokenness* that remains to be fixed, it truly is our dream home. After moving around every three years, the memories that our children are building in this home as they finally get to settle down are priceless.

I get it; I really do. At the end of the day, who cares! It's just a building, right? Yes, it is. So what about those three stinking screws? If I understand and believe everything I have shared with you in this book, how in the world do *three screws* have the power to cause such difficult moments? Well, because we forget that while we have experienced healing (Isaiah 53:5), there is this brokenness that remains.

After four years of big expenses, we are finally getting to do some of the cosmetic projects that we dreamed about. Since our boys have officially entered the teenage years, and our daughter has entered the big kid/pre-teen years, a big part of their Christmas gifts this year was to do their rooms in a way that represents who they really are. After all, they've had different rooms every three years since the day they were born and never complained about it.

For our sweet Elli, there was not a lot to be done. She wanted her room's theme to go from a "little girl's farm" to a "big girl on a safari through Africa." A new color of paint, bedding, a new and fully restored writing desk found at the Salvation Army Thrift Store (now *she* wants to be a writer), and... "Safari through Africa" it is!

The boys' room required more time, effort, and a little bit more funding than their sister's room did. Their room was mostly labor intensive, aside from the paint and three screws. Ok, more than three screws, but three screws are what we are talking about here.

After I finished painting Caleb's bed, his side of the room was all ready to go and be put back together. But the brokenness that remained would start rearing its ugly head with these three screws necessary to secure part of the base. The bed only required three screws, but their positioning was crucial for the stability of our strong and growing teenage boy's bed. Now, I am the dreamer, the visionary, and the painter. My man is the one who knows where the screws go for something to stand securely. So, I needed his help.

The fact that I needed him was not the problem, and I hope you are starting to see that the three screws were not the problem, either. No, the problem was the timing of my asking for his help (Ok, my *telling* him to help) because it triggered some of the *brokenness that remains* from past experiences in each of our individual lives that had an effect early in our marriage. My man had no sooner walked in the door, when in my excitement I said, "Great! You are home! I need you to carry this board upstairs and secure it to the wall for Caleb's bed. All you need are three screws. Thank you!" And off I went in another direction.

Sweet friend, I don't even think I said "Hi" to the man who had just arrived home at the end of a very long, busy week at work. Now my intent was never to communicate to him that I didn't care or appreciate him and all he does for our family, because Lord knows I do appreciate him. But despite my intentions, with good motives and all, that was exactly what my words and my actions said to him.

Well, he did carry the board and the screws upstairs. But then he sat down with the kids to watch a movie. When I made this discovery, I not so very gently asked, "What about the board?" To which he not so gently said, "I am tired. It was a long week and a long drive home. Can't I just relax and get to it in the morning?"

Maybe you already know where this is heading. Maybe not.

"Don't you care?" I thought. "I have been working my tail off on this project so I can save us money." But don't be fooled by my thoughts. While that was true, the truth is that I actually enjoy doing these projects. It provides a great outlet for my creativity and gives me breathing space in the middle of a writing deadline. All I needed was ten minutes of his time to put three screws in the wall for me. I would take care of the rest! I thought that was a pretty good deal. But instead, he was feeling unappreciated, wondering if I cared how tired he was and how hard he was working to provide for us.

I think it is safe to say that most of you can see both of our viewpoints. You may relate to one more than the other, but the points are valid in both accounts. Could *we* see both viewpoints? No, neither one of us could. We were distracted by both being tired and by the *brokenness that remains* from our past (with which we are very much at peace). If we are not careful, this brokenness will sneak up on us, often during projects around the house when we are tired. During these times, our own selfishness blinds us from seeing the other's point of view.

Yes, I should have said that the project could wait until the morning. But I just wanted the task completed so I could move on from it. These three pathetic screws were the only thing holding me back. Yes, looking back, I could have waited. But that required me dying to self.

Yes, he can now see that while I may know he would rather have no projects on a Friday night when he gets home from work late, taking the time to complete a very simple task involving three screws was something that could have been done quickly and without much effort. Yes, looking back he could have just done it quickly and then lay down to watch a movie with the kids and relax for the rest of the night. But you see, that would require him dying to self also.

On this Friday night, when we were both tired, frustrated, and feeling unappreciated by the other, all we wanted was for the other one to die to self. With this mindset, we lost sight of what was happening and how pathetic we were both acting. It clearly was not about the three screws. But these three screws represented the hurt and the brokenness that remained from some of our past experiences.

> We often make the mistake of thinking that because past brokenness has been healed and restored, it no longer has an effect on how we respond when the weather shifts and we are tired.

We often make the mistake of thinking that because past brokenness has been healed and restored, it no longer has an effect on how we respond when the weather shifts and we are tired. Instead of acknowledging our shortcomings, pride jumps back in, and we get lost in pointing fingers. We pick at old wounds, wondering if we really are at peace with the brokenness at all. We keep tripping over these things because we start to shove the brokenness that remains under the rug. Because this brokenness will remain until Jesus comes back, it's difficult to endure, and remaining at peace in it requires effort. For example, even though all the details of my stories didn't make it onto the pages of this book, it doesn't mean each story doesn't have to be sifted through in this process of writing. As a result, my heart has visited some difficult places. That is the reason why each and every chapter of this book has been the most difficult one to write...yet.

Because God has healed and restored my past, and because I am able to be at peace with it, means it is well with my soul. But it doesn't mean that I don't have to keep my heart in check when life takes unexpected turns, or when I have to wait for three pathetic screws to secure a board to the wall. (The bed is up, and the boys' room is finished, by the way.)

As you can see, because the *brokenness that remains* can sometimes sneak up on us, it is crucial that we don't walk the journey alone. It is crucial that we surround ourselves with God-given friendships which I often refer to as *life-giving*. But we need to start by *being* the life-giving friend we need for the remainder of our journey.

After that three screw incident, I realized I needed to take a break from my isolated writing corner and meet with one of my wiser-than-me friends. I needed accountability. Writing deadlines can be difficult because they are very isolating for me. Now the isolation is not as horrible as how raw some emotions can feel when I visit the difficult places and the brokenness God has delivered me from. The writing process requires me to revisit these difficult places of my journey in order for God to sift my heart and give me the words to share His story of redemption, the story of His peace in my life. People are often surprised to find out that I am actually a homebody at heart. I am not as extroverted as some people would think I am. And I am okay with that. So the *being home* is not what is difficult. And as tough as it may be to go to these difficult places during such an isolating time, I treasure these times with God.

But it would be foolish of me not to realize that it is also during those times when I am tired and emotions are raw that I am extremely vulnerable. During those times, Satan, the enemy of my soul, is very much aware of it. He stands by patiently for opportunities such as the three screws to present themselves and shake things up a bit. Writing down words in a book is not easy, but if we seek Him, He will give us the words. So even though this book has my name on it, I am fully aware of Who gave it to me. While this writing journey requires discipline, reflection, and deep study of Scripture, writing the words is not terribly difficult either. Now, living out my message? Ha! Yeah, that is where it gets difficult because the words that I write down (or speak) should be a reflection of how I live and what I am living for. That right there is why having life-giving friends is crucial. I needed some encouragement and accountability. It was time to take a small break from writing and reach out. I reached out to one of my wiser-than-me friends to see if we could catch up.

So as my wiser-than-me friend and I got caught up in life, we both shared things we needed prayer for. Now, we have been friends long enough and know enough about each other's stories that details are not always needed. But here is where I had to say more than just, "please pray that I will finish this last chapter by the deadline." Even though that is a very heartfelt prayer right now (who knew that writing the last half of this last chapter would take so long and be so difficult?), my prayer needed to include the pathetic "three screws in the wall" story. I was able to briefly share that I was physically tired, my heart was a little tired, too, from the sifting process, and my emotions had gotten the best of me.

My friend heard me out as she usually does. She shared some encouragement, and she told me how proud she was of me for continuing to move forward in obedience, especially when it was difficult. But my friend's encouragement also included, in not so many words, a reminder to get my heart back to the cross and keep my emotions in check. That is what makes her a good life-giving friend.

So how do we find that kind of friendship—the friendship we *all* long for? That question right there is in part what makes writing *this* last chapter so difficult. I can't tell you that if you read this chapter, you will end up with the friendships you have always wanted. It just doesn't work that way. That's what makes it so difficult to write this message. What I can tell you is that the friendships we long for can be found because, just like peace, they are God-given. But we must be sensitive to God's Holy Spirit and pay close attention when He points them out.

The last friendship I just shared with you came about as I was walking down a hallway at church one day. God must have shown her something; He must have whispered to her heart, encouraging her to reach out to me. And I am so glad that she was obedient. She is one of the most remarkable women I know. She has a way of encouraging my heart while asking the difficult questions. And that is exactly what she did that day. But here is the thing, she welcomes the same difficult questions from me and is not afraid to reach out when it's her turn to do so.

As a matter of fact, she did just that a few days ago. I got a text, and this time it was her asking if I could meet her. She had just stepped into some difficult obedience. You know, the kind of obedience that while we know it will bring about something wonderful, the first steps are tough to make, and they require sacrifice. Yes, even good steps that we know will bring about something great are difficult to take when the very next step is all you can see, and God says that is time to take it. So even though she is a wiser-than-me friend, it was her turn to be encouraged, prayed for, and yes, held accountable to just keep taking the next step in front of her. It was my turn to encourage her and be a life-giving friend.

So if we all long for those kinds of friendships, what makes them so difficult to find? I believe the answer is two-fold...maybe even three-fold; we'll see where God takes us.

The first reason why it is difficult to find those life-giving friendships is because we romanticize friendships. We make the tragic mistake of thinking that every friendship needs to reach the same intimate depth and level of sharing our hearts in order to be a great friendship. The truth is that it just can't be that way. We may walk different parts of our journey with different wonderful, life-giving friends. But for the friendship to reach that level of intimacy where we don't have to go back and explain the details in our lives in order for them to get it, those friendships take time to develop. There is just no way around it.

> The first reason why it is difficult to find those life-giving friendships is because we romanticize friendships.

The second reason it's difficult for us to find those life-giving friendships is the expectations we put on them. After all, friendships bring us great joy, companionship, and encouragement. However, when motives are not kept in check and the expectations we put on friendships are not met, those friendships can also be where we experience deep wounds. I believe that much like peace, we have allowed our broken world to define our view and expectations of friendship.

I am sure you have heard the saying, "Tell me who your friends are, and I'll tell you who you are." Yes, there is a lot of truth in that statement. However, I am going to suggest that we need to play with the order of the words a little. I think it should be more like, "Tell me who you are, and it will tell me about your friends."

Remember, in order to have the type of friendship we desire, *we* need to be that friend first—the one with whom we want to be friends! We need to stop being defined by the friendships we want. And we need to start letting the way we live our lives define our friendships. We need to stop comparing our friendships to what the world defines as "popular."

Life-giving friendships have to start with us first. We need to be the friend who breathes life *into* people's lives instead of sucking the life *out of* them. We need to stop expecting for our friendships (or any relationship for that matter) to meet all our needs. When we forget that Jesus is the only one who can meet all our needs, our genuine need for friendships turns into *neediness*.

When we continually put our burdens onto someone else, we are no longer known as a *life-giving friend*. Instead of walking alongside each other, helping to carry each other's burdens to the foot of the cross, we become *burden-giving* friends. We must remember at all times that Jesus is the only One who can meet all of our needs. If we don't catch ourselves, we will end up belly flopping into our pit thinking, "If I only had the right friends. If only my circumstances were different..." all over again.

Oh, how I wish I could only write about *those* friends, you know, the burden-giving ones. But unfortunately, I have been that friend. Trust me, having been given that extra million set of emotions that need to be kept in check, I understand how easy it is to become *that* friend. When my emotions have gotten the best of me, I have been a *burden-giving friend* by processing my brokenness to death, really getting stuck on it. I understand that it can seem so much easier to share and bring brokenness to a friend instead of taking it to the foot of the cross and giving it to the only One who can meet all of our needs. I understand that when we take it to the foot of the cross, we can't talk our way out of why *that* burden is not the one that needs to be laid down. I understand we can't argue that God is wrong when we don't agree with what He reveals to us. Well, I mean, we can, but it doesn't change the fact that He is God, and we are not. It doesn't change the fact that His will *will* be done and whether it is what we want or not, our peace will only be found when, like Jesus, in humility we say, "Father, if you are willing, remove this cup from me. Nevertheless, not my will, but yours, be done" (Luke 22:42). It is well with my soul.

Because I understand how quickly I can become a burden-giving friend instead of a life-giving one, I've had to learn to keep my needs from becoming needy. So I have developed a system that helps me out. The system consists of a small group of girlfriends (they don't even know who each other are) that when it's time for me to get my heart to the cross, I will send a short text saying, "on my way to the cross" or in emergency situations like in the dressing room in Chapter Two, one of my friends will get this text: "Help! I have belly flopped into my own pit, please pray me back." And sometimes all I can get out is "please pray."

Either way, just like in the dressing room, the reply is simple, "I am on it," or "Praying." Period. It has to be that simple. Then I can stay focused and take *all* of my emotions to the only One who can handle them. Instead of dumping all of those emotions on my friends, I go to the cross. I know that as my heart wrestles, I have a sister praying for me, praying that in my brokenness, I will finally say, "Not my will, but Your will be done. I surrender! I will seek Your kingdom first and trust You for the rest." If my friend doesn't get a text back from me at some point saying, "I am back," she will send me a text asking me if I am. The next time I see her, I know she will look at me straight in the eyes and ask me, "Are you really back?" My answer will be a simple "yes" or "no." Once my answer is "yes," then we can talk about it.

Here is why it has to be that way: because then I can share with her what God has shown my heart according to His Word. Instead of putting the burden on my friend, I have given my burden to God. Then my friend can help me check to make sure it lines up with scripture, and I can ask that friend to hold me accountable to continue to surrender to His will even when it is difficult.

That is what happened when I met with my friend after the three screws incident. By the time I met with her, I didn't share with her the details of the three screws or my wrestling with God about what the three screws represented. No. I was able to share how God had shown me that I needed rest and to keep my emotions in check. She was then able to encourage me and hold me accountable to what God had shown me, to keep getting my heart back to the cross in order to keep my emotions in check. She told me she would be committed to praying for me, and she would text me to check in with me at the end of the week.

Listen, I must tell you this, all my life-giving friends to whom I have been a burden-giving friend instead of a life-giving friend, that last paragraph has become music to their ears! The reward that awaits them in heaven is indescribable. They have endured, loved, asked the really difficult questions, held me accountable, and prayed me out of some nasty pity parties. You can thank them for their faithfulness, endurance, and prayers. Because it took me going through that process in order to share what I have learned with you on the pages of this book.

Sweet friend-, there is nothing romantic about those friendships. And God knows if they had known the mess I can be when the brokenness that remains sneaks up on me, they would not have chosen me nor I them! Yes, they are wonderful, but they have required time and effort. Is it worth the investment? Absolutely! Because I have been willing to risk being vulnerable with this group of friends, they are able to be vulnerable with me, and now I get the same texts from them. As a result we have become life-giving friends to *each other*. And trust me; there is no brokenness I won't walk through with them.

I understand the longing to be known as well as to know someone. However, the life-giving friendships that I have shared with you will require us being present right where we are, in the season we currently are in, with people who have access to our lives, and with people God has identified.

Ok, that last part is huge! Not everyone who has given us access to *their* lives or who has access to *our* lives is meant to be a life-giving friend with access to the same depth as the ones God has identified as such. It just doesn't work that way. If we get stuck in having the friend we *want* to have and don't keep our neediness and our motives in check, we can easily—and even without knowing—manipulate circumstances that will give us access to someone who gains access to our lives just for the sake of getting close. That can happen when a gymnastic class is picked so there is a chance to end up in the waiting area with that person. Or when someone offers to serve in a ministry in order to have a closer view into your life and vice versa. You get the point. If we are not careful, we will manipulate situations in our lives (intentionally or not) to have the friendships that we *want* instead of seeking the ones ordained and *given* by God.

Let me share a story that paints a picture of a *God-given friendship*. I had the wonderful blessing of being part of the women's ministry staff at a church in Michigan some years ago. The story I am going to share happened a few months after I joined the ministry team.

My friend's office was the place where everyone knew they could stop by and find some kind of chocolate or candy. I am sure that to this day, her office remains that place where people sneak in during those *emergency* chocolate moments in ministry. But this friend is so much more than the "sweet tooth" fairy in the office; she is a crucial part of the administrative support team for the church. Since administration is not one of my strong suits, I kind of require a little more time during any new database training sessions. Well, my friend's office is one of the first stops in training. I needed to learn the database system (sweet mercy!) and that is her area of expertise.

Because it takes a couple of times for my brain to catch up with this kind of training, I found myself needing to stop by her office more often than not (and not just for the chocolate).

I was sitting in her training chair during one of my frequent visits to her office to ask a question about the system…again. When we were finally finished, I finally had all of my "handy dandy" notes to complete my tasks. As I was getting ready to get up and leave her office, she smiled and said, "You know, I didn't want to love you!"

I smiled, sat back down in her training chair, and said, "Tell me more about that," to which she answered:

"Well, the first time I saw you I was like, 'Good Lord, who is this happy, full of life, with a smile on her face and always ready-to-give-a-hug chick that just walked in the office?' to which God said, 'You are going to have to love her.' I told God that I didn't want to and that you didn't need me. But God was persistent. As annoyed as I was with how happy, giggly, and full of energy you were, every time you walked into my office, I became intrigued by your life story. So, I finally decided to listen and obey God. Well, come to find out, God didn't want me to be friends with you because of you. I am the one who received the blessing. As I've heard your story, I have been blessed to be part of something bigger than myself by seeing God's story in your life. I have been blessed by seeing first-hand how God heals, how God loves, and how God brings peace in the midst of suffering, in the brokenness. Gina, the crazy thing is that after all this time I've had to spend with you sitting in my training chair, seeing all that God has done, now I actually love you! I guess it's not all about us. It's about how God will use us to bless others and ultimately bring glory to the One who loves us always unconditionally."

I smiled back and said "HA! I love it when He does that! Thank you for being obedient and loving me. I am sure it's just a matter of time before I am going to need that kind of love, a God given love. And PS, I love you right back." While I don't get to see her as often now, that was the beginning of a friendship I still treasure deeply. Oh, and believe me, the time did come when I would need her to love *me*…more than once.

Of all the stories I could share with you, why that one? Because it is the one that communicates best what happens when God picks our friendships instead of us wanting to always pick who our friends are. I asked my friend if I could share our story, and when she emailed me back, she closed her email with, "Sometimes God brings people in our lives, and we have no idea why. Or we make the excuse that we don't have the time or energy. God has an amazing way to use us, always for our good and His glory."

God-given friendships, the ones that our hearts long for, don't just happen; we don't always get to pick the friendships we want. They are just that, God-given. And they usually come in the least expected way with unexpected people.

I wonder if you are asking yourself what in the world do God-given friendships have to do with peace? A lot, actually. While the only One needed for peace is Jesus, I hope that as I have shared my heart with you and what God has shown me in this adventure and journey of finding *Peace in the Brokenness*, I hope that you have noticed I have not walked this journey alone. You shouldn't either. Nobody should. We were never meant to walk alone. We are relational beings created in the image of a relational God. Throughout Scripture we read examples of the friend who has stuck closer than a brother (or sister). And that is why this chapter is so important. God given friendships are the tool God uses to help us walk through the brokenness that will remain on this Genesis 3 world we live in.

God-given friendships are recorded all throughout Scripture. In the Old Testament, we read about friendships such as David and Jonathan (1 Samuel). In the book of Ruth, we read the story of the unlikely and unexpected friendship between Ruth and Naomi. And in the book of Ecclesiastes we read that "two are better than one" (Ecclesiastes 4:9).

As we move into the New Testament, we read about Jesus, God in the flesh, becoming our friend when He tells us so in John 15:15, "No longer do I call you servants, for the servant does not know what his master is doing; but I have called you friends, for all that I have heard from my Father I have made known to you." We spend much of the Gospels reading about what those friendships look like through the life of Jesus and His disciples. We talked in depth about one of my favorite friendship stories with Jesus in Chapter Three through the story of Martha, Mary, and their brother Lazarus.

As we move through the rest of the New Testament, another one of my favorite stories is the one of Barnabas and Paul found in Acts 11. And through much of Paul's writings, we often read about Paul's friendship with Timothy. There are simply way too many friendships to mention. We will take a closer look at what these friendships look like at the end of the chapter during our last homework exercise. I would encourage you to take a closer look at the friendships throughout the Bible. There is much to be learned about them.

Remember, the first reason it's difficult to find these life-giving friendships is that we have romanticized what friendships look like. The second reason is we put too many expectations on those friendships to be the ones that meet all of our needs instead of helping us carry our burdens to the cross through prayer. So the third reason is that much like everything else, we have allowed the world to define what friendships should look like.

It doesn't require much thought to determine that one of the current, leading problems romanticizing and distorting friendships is social media. We are concerned with how many followers our friends have, how many likes they get on their post, or the pictures of them having dinners, parties, coffee dates, and lunches with other friends. I don't think it would take long before I get an "Amen" to that. However, we really need to make a couple corrections to that statement as well. I believe it is more accurate to say that the leading problems distorting friendships is our *unhealthy boundaries* in the world of social media. Sweet friend, we simply can't blame social media. Social media is just a tool. *How we use it* determines if it is a problem or not.

Remember, life-giving friendships come with the good, the not-so-great, and everything in between. Social media does not capture every area or moment in our lives—and it shouldn't! (By the way, dirty laundry needs to be kept in the laundry room.) Social media posts and pictures are simply snapshots of life. Yes, friendships are captured in these pictures. But the only way to get a full view into someone's life is to *be a part of it*, life on life. And we soon forget that there is a huge difference between a life-giving friend and a *follower*. When we allow social media to define our understanding of friendships, we forget that posts and pictures are simply snapshots of their day. And when we forget that this isn't the big picture of their lives, the ever-so-destructive comparison game begins. Instead, we should take responsibility for our emotions and ask ourselves a more difficult question: "Why does this bother me?"

I had to ask myself that question not too long ago. Remember I said that writing deadlines can become somewhat isolating for me? Yes, there are only so many hours in a day, and during this season I have to be super intentional and careful of where my time is spent. As a result,

I had to keep saying no to invitations from friends. They completely understood and have cheered me on all along. However, that didn't keep them from going on with their lives and having fun without me. And it most certainly shouldn't have! But I would be lying to you if, after seeing picture after picture of them having fun, I didn't start having "hmmm" moments in my mind. In their effort to be sensitive and supportive to my deadlines, they stopped asking me to join them. In addition to my "hmmm" thoughts, my insecurities started rearing their ugly heads at this point. You know, I started wondering if my friends had moved on in life without me, and I wondered if they even noticed that I was not there with them.

But I had to stop the madness! I could do one of three things: I could either keep belly flopping into my own pit of insecurities; I could say, "Whatever!" or I could grow up, own my insecurities, and let them know I missed them and couldn't wait to come out and play again.

Well, the very next day we had just left church when I got a text from a friend that said, "Hey! I went to look for you, but you had left already. Are you guys up to meeting us for lunch?" I smiled, read it to my man, and we went. It wasn't super long because I did have a deadline to meet. But I was able to share my heart with my friend and how much I had missed her. It was great. Here is the thing, if I had not stopped to ask myself what it was that was bothering me, I would not have been able to put words to it and share my heart with my friends. It would have seemed easier to shove it under the rug and keep tripping over it... but not this time.

Sweet friend, social media does not show the depth of the *brokenness that remains.* I get it. Is it supposed to? I don't think so, at least not from the point of the scriptures. Public spaces are not the place to share the details or the depth of our struggles. And Jesus didn't invite the crowds to go with Him in Luke 22:42. As a matter of fact, He didn't even invite

His entire small group of twelve disciples. No, He only invited three: Peter, John, and James.

When we lose sight of the purpose of public spaces in our lives, we think we are the only one who struggles with the brokenness that remains. When we mistake the number of "followers" in our public spaces for real life-giving friends, we get ourselves into trouble.

Sweet friend, we must make it a point to keep our own hearts in check *before* we complain on social media platforms and even before we blame social media for our own brokenness. We either need to understand how large public spaces work and set up healthy boundaries, or we need to stay out of them altogether. I would recommend setting healthy boundaries, be it on social media or in any other type of public space. The beauty in all of this is that we have a choice; no social media platform or physical public space has the power to remove our peace unless we allow it to do so. We must not give in to comparing our lives with others.

We must always remember, as great as someone else's social media life may look, for the most part, they would be the first ones to tell you that their posts are simply snapshots of their day. I know there have been a couple of times after I posted an angelic picture of one of my children when I have completely lost my mind for a minute or two. There was a time that after I posted a picture of a pretty dinner plate, actually as I was hitting "post," my dog licked my plate! Listen, we must learn to move on from allowing others' insecurities to bring up our own. And we need to be happy for other people having happy moments! We must keep our heart and all our feelings in check. In order to do so, we will need life-giving friends to encourage us. After I shared with my friend how I was feeling, she was so glad I did. I still couldn't go out to play much yet, but we were more intentional about staying connected in real life.

Ok, enough about social media and public spaces. Let's move on to the kind of friendships needed on our journey to peace in the brokenness that remains: God-given friendships, life-on-life kind of friendships! My hope is that this chapter will encourage you in knowing that like peace, true friendships *can* be found. But much like peace, in order to find the true, long lasting friendships, we must look at the model we see in Scripture.

I think it is important to be reminded that not every friendship is meant to reach the same level or depth as the next friendship in order to be a life-giving one that we enjoy and value. If we remind ourselves of that, we will be better prepared to keep expectations in check.

During the years of Jesus' public ministry, He had large crowds following Him. Yes, they got to interact and have community together, because they were in the same public spaces already. These are the friends we see mainly at gatherings or when we run into each other around town. These are the people we are genuinely happy to see, and with whom we have a pleasant conversation. We may even count them as good friends because they are. We may not see each other much, but we genuinely care for them and their wellbeing, and they care for us, too. There just isn't enough life happening together to be able to invest further. But they are good friends nonetheless.

Then we have Jesus' *small group*: the twelve disciples. This group knew a lot more details of Jesus' life because they were walking closer with Him. They were doing life together; they were in ministry with Him, serving alongside Him. Scripture doesn't say this, but I am sure that this group knew Him well enough that they could have finished some of His sentences. These were the friends who, if one of the disciples had kids and the babysitter canceled last minute on the night of something big, he would have called Jesus or any one of the disciples without hesitation to see if they could keep the kids. They were that close.

That is where most people usually stop as far as friendships. However, I believe that those deep relationships we all long for are better illustrated with the three close friends whom Jesus invited to join Him in the moments when Jesus' heart had more than it could bear. Jesus invited Peter, John, and James to go with Him to the Garden of Gethsemane when He needed to go and pour His heart out to the Father and give Him the things that had become overwhelming, burdensome, and sorrowful to His soul. They were present at the moment when nothing but time with the Father would do, and it was time to get back to the Father, the only One who had the answers (Matthew 26:36–38).

In that passage, we read that Jesus invited His three closest friends to go with Him, to wait for Him, to watch, and to pray while He went to the Father. For us today, I call those moments "getting to the cross" since that is how we have access to God the Father, through His Son's payment on the cross.

In the passage of Mathew 26, we read that He asked His three closest friends to stay close and pray for Him. He knew that they had reached the point in which He needed to bring His heart only to the Father. As His friends sat back and prayed, Jesus went a little further. He "fell on his face and prayed, saying, 'My Father, if it be possible, let this cup pass from me; nevertheless, not as I will, but as you will.' And he came to the disciples and found them sleeping. And he said to Peter, 'So, could you not watch with me one hour?'" (Matthew 26:39–40).

When our friends do not meet our needs, we could probably ask the same question. We could even stomp off wounded and belly flop into a pity party about it. But Jesus doesn't do that. No, Jesus knows that while He longs for those friends to pray for Him in His greatest time of need, His own needs can only be met by the Father. He could have told His friends to get lost and then hold a grudge against them; certainly we would all understand. But no, Jesus doesn't do that because scripture is very clear. He asked His friends to keep praying for Him each time

He went back to the Father. He asked them to watch and to pray three times (to be exact) as He went back to His Father, asking if there was any other way for His will to be done. Wait! Jesus asked the Father the same question three times? Yes, because in His human form, Jesus was overwhelmed by the task ahead of Him.

Jesus was overwhelmed by the plan of the Father, the only plan that would work. Yeah, I often wonder if Jesus ever shared a better plan with the Father to bring peace to our restlessness. We don't know the details of that conversation. What we do know is that Jesus, in His human form, wrestled with the physical and spiritual brokenness that was coming ahead. But He was the only one who could carry out the plan for salvation to bring us peace. So even though Jesus asked the Father if there was any other way, three times, He ultimately submitted to the will of the Father, and we must do the same in order to be at peace.

Sweet friend, we must understand that in His moment of *brokenness*, Jesus didn't overcome the weight of the burden because He is God. He didn't overcome and surrender to the Father's will out of His deity. No, in that moment of pain, in that moment of being overwhelmed with the burden of our brokenness He came to pay for, Jesus overcame His brokenness, because He came to do the will of the Father. He listened only to the words of the Father. Therefore, He overcame that moment because He submitted to the will of the Father.

Jesus knew all along why He had come: to die for us. But in that moment, in His human form, when the plan is more than His heart can bear, when His heart is overwhelmed to the point of death as He feels the sorrow that is ahead, Jesus submits to the will of the Father and "for the joy that was set before him endured the cross, despising the shame" (Hebrews 12:2).

What was the joy set before Him you ask? *You!* You are the joy set before Him. He knew that His death and resurrection would bring restoration to our brokenness. We, too, can overcome the enemy of our souls in times of temptation, or we can choose whatever the apple in Genesis 3 represents in our lives today. Scripture says, "They overcame him [the enemy of our souls and the apples in our lives] by the blood of the Lamb and because of the word of their testimony" (Revelation 12:11).

So now that we got a glimpse into the brokenness that Jesus must have been feeling and was overwhelmed by, we can understand why He had brought and asked His three closest friends to pray for Him. But what about those three friends? Yeah, they were Jesus' three closest friends, *and* they fell asleep! We read of Jesus' frustration when He asked them if they could not just pray for one hour. But we don't read of Jesus stomping off or holding a grudge against them. No, to the contrary, He said, "Rise, let us be going; see, my betrayer is at hand" (Matthew 26:46). Jesus didn't trade His friends' brokenness for other *better* friends. No, He invited them to walk with Him, even though He could have justified feeling betrayed by Peter, John, and James during His time of need. But Jesus didn't do that. Jesus kept His expectations on the Father. After all, the will of the Father is what Jesus came to fulfill.

It is difficult not to hold grudges when our closest friends disappoint us by falling asleep during our greatest times of need. But I believe that if we keep our expectations at the foot of the cross and trust our hearts and our brokenness to the only One who can fill that God-shaped hole in our hearts, we *can* find peace. God will never—no, not ever—leave us. He will never let go of us. He will never fall asleep on us. I believe that by keeping our expectations in check, our friends will be freed to walk the journey with us without the pressure or expectation that they are the ones who will meet all our needs or help us process our brokenness to death . We will be free to do what God intended us to do in our friendships: to help each other carry our burdens to the foot of Jesus' cross. Then we, too, can overcome our trials through the blood of the Lamb.

When we choose to be the friend who is *life-giving* instead of *burden-giving*, we find those sweet God-given friendships that He has in store for us, the kind of friendship for which we long. God will grant us the life-giving friend we need to walk the journey with us while we seek, choose, and hold on to His peace in the brokenness that remains.

But I think there is a fourth reason that makes those friendships difficult to find. This one feels very vulnerable to me. The fourth reason is that we often say we want to be held accountable and that we want to be teachable, but if we get really honest, sometimes we just want someone to tell us how great we are doing. Or as one of my wiser-than-me friends would say, "someone to tickle our ears" and agree with us. I think most of us can understand that. Yes, we need those friends who will encourage us and cheer us on in the areas we are getting right. However, if they are going to be life-giving friends, they also need to love us enough to ask the difficult questions, even if our feelings may get hurt.

I have been on both sides of that situation. I have been on the side of having to accept that even though God had shown me something, it wasn't time for me to share it. My friend was not ready to hear the difficult questions, at least not from me or not at that moment. As challenging as that was, I needed to be okay with that. Listen friends, just because God reveals something to us about another person's brokenness does not mean we have to call them out, just to call them out. When we do that, I believe we cause more damage than help. When we call out for the sake of calling out, we only add to their brokenness. As difficult as it is to see someone in need and not be able to do anything for them, and as noble as our motives may be, I have learned that sometimes God shows us others' brokenness so we can be quietly on our knees, praying diligently for them while God is stirring their hearts. Sometimes he doesn't want us to jump in and rescue them.

The Brokenness That Remains | 155

Life-giving friendships are not meant to rescue. Life-giving friends are the tool that God uses to help us keep walking in the midst of the brokenness that remains. Life giving friendships are the tool that points us to the only One who can rescue us. They point us to the Savior, the Prince of Peace, Jesus.

Life-giving friendships are not meant to rescue. Life-giving friends are the tool that God uses to help us keep walking in the midst of the brokenness that remains.

I am sure we probably all have been there at one point—that point when the brokenness is piling up on us or on our friends. In those moments, it is crucial that we rely completely in the leading of the Holy Spirit. This was beautifully modeled to me by one of my wiser-than-me friends. Remember that conference where I cried all of my mascara and make up off? The one where God did major open heart surgery in the middle of a large auditorium full of strangers by reminding me of the dreams that He had given me? Yeah, that one. Well after that I shared what God had shown me with another wiser-than-me friend (different from the one who drove me there). As I am sharing with her, her eyes start filling up with tears while her smile starts getting bigger. Her response was simple but powerful. She simply said, "You have no idea the prayers that I have been praying for you, my sweet girl."

Ok, confession. That sounded very romantic, right? Now, don't misunderstand me here. It was beautiful. It was powerful. It was however, a little confusing to me. This wiser-than-me friend has more access to my heart and my life than most people. She has earned that place of trust and can ask me any difficult question she wants, and she has. She has asked me some of the most difficult questions in my journey to peace, questions like, "What does peace look like here, Gina?" when each one of the boxes in my heart would burst open and the brokenness would be exposed.

Can you see why I was a bit confused? Maybe not. I was confused because I just didn't understand why she would not have shared those prayers with me. Why didn't she tell me what she was seeing? So with a combination of confusion and a hint of frustration I asked her that, "Why didn't you tell me? Why didn't you stop me?" In her very sweet, but firm way, she responded by telling me that she tried, but I wouldn't hear it. So she stopped asking, not because she was afraid to hurt my feelings and risk the friendship, but because God would have to be the One to show me.

No, it wasn't that she was afraid to hurt my feelings or take the risk. We know this is true because she was the one who told me she could see that I was hurting. She told me that she adored me. She told me that she would walk the journey with me. But let's not forget that right after giving me that very sweet and tender encouragement, she also spoke a difficult to hear truth when she said that she wasn't interested in my head answers anymore, and neither was God.

Yeah, looking back, she had tried asking me the difficult questions. I remember a very specific time when she asked me if I was done running from the dreams God had given me. I think I gave her one of my Camp Cynical answers. Something like, "Yeah, I am working on that. I have a lot on my plate right now." I remember her asking me if I was ready to talk about it. I once again replied with a cynical and sarcastic tone when I said, "No, thank you."

Ah! Sweet friend-, my heart can be such an ugly and messy place at times. I was so consumed by my brokenness and so busy trying to please and meet other people's expectations of me that I couldn't even hear the questions she was asking. I was so busy belly flopping into my pit of "if only's" that I just couldn't see it. I am sure she would have loved to say to God that she was done with me. Maybe she did. But God-given friendships don't work like that. I am sure there must have been times when she went to the cross and she must have prayed, "Is there anyone else who can walk her through this? Is there any way you can remove this cup from me?"

She has never said that to me, by the way. I don't know what her prayers to the Father were about me. All I know is that at some point she must have said, "Your will be done" and at that moment, while I am sure she may have wanted to shake me and call me out in efforts to rescue me from some of the brokenness that she could see coming, she knew it was not her job to rescue me, but to keep praying to the only One who could. She submitted to the will of the Father and continued to wear out her knees and heart on my behalf. She stayed close by and kept asking the only question I could hear because it was what I was in desperate search of, "What does peace look like here, Gina." Then she would send me off to the cross to get the answer. And that is what makes her a life-giving friend: her commitment was first to the kingdom of God. She was all about "the Father's business" even when it involved the risk of having to ask the difficult questions. As a result we've had the blessing of walking some long valleys and celebrating some incredibly beautiful mountain tops.

So why did she ask me the question and not just give me the answers? Yes, she could have just given me the answer. She is very much aware of what peace has looked like in many seasons of life. But that is not how life-giving friendships works. In order for us to be able to fully embrace peace in the brokenness of this Genesis 3 world we leave in, we must constantly make room in our lives to be still and know that He is God. It will require constantly seeking His kingdom first and trusting Him for the rest. It will require remaining in Him so that His peace can remain in us. It will require the laying down of anything that gets in the way of our seeking Him with all our hearts. When we do seek Him with all our hearts, He will be found, and He will show us the good and full of hope dreams that He has for us. It will require doing our homework in order to have quality time with Him instead of simply checking off our homework boxes. And here is the thing, it will require us being willing to be that life-giving friend *first* so we can better identify our God-given friendships. We must be the kind of friend we all long for and need. If we are going to walk the journey and be at peace in the brokenness that will remain, we must be a life-giving friend until Jesus returns or calls us home.

Well, to this day, I don't know the details of what my wiser-than-me friend's prayers were for me in that season. But I am sure they had to do with God's dream for me in writing this book. How do I know that? Well, I am sitting here at two o'clock in the morning with an overflowing heart and thankful tears, wondering how in the world did I get here! What started out as me journaling the answers to her question, "What does peace look like here, Gina?" has turned into a book, and I am writing the last chapter right now. Only God! Everything about this book can only be described by God. I am just a simple woman who decided to lay it all down at the foot of the cross. With my identity finally secured in Him alone, I dared to dream bigger than ever before for my God. When He showed me the dream of this book, I had no idea what He would do with it or where it would end.

> I am just a simple woman who decided to lay it all down at the foot of the cross. With my identity finally secured in Him alone, I dared to dream bigger than ever before for my God.

With my heart beating fast and trembling knees before my God, I said, "Yes, Lord! Whatever You want. Because even 'if not', You are still good because You are God." The journey has been long and at times really messy. But I made a promise to my God when I was 21 years old sitting by myself in the middle of a rug-less floor in a small and empty apartment. After everything He had delivered me from, I promised Him that if He chose to use my brokenness for His kingdom, I would do whatever I could to encourage women to seek Him with all their heart and find Him. I promised Him that I would do whatever I could for the advancement of His kingdom and for women to know that they don't have to walk life and the brokenness alone. Well, this book is just me keeping my promise. He is the One who has closed and open doors. Yes, it has been a long and messy journey. Has it been worth it? You better believe it! My God is worthy, and His kingdom is worth every moment along this journey.

So last confession. I sat here for about fifteen minutes, staring at my screen since I typed that last sentence. I am pleading with God to give me the words. I have done that since before I sat down to write the very first word in Chapter One. But this is different. We have come to the end of our time together. How in the world does one wrap up six chapters of writing in the next two to three paragraphs? How in the world do I convey to you how very dear you have become to my heart? Truth is, I am feeling little bit stuck.

So how is God answering my prayer this time? By reminding me of a text I got from my editor a few months back when I was feeling stuck, and I was not sure if I was going to meet a deadline (very much like I am feeling right at this moment). "Concentrate on the woman holding your book in the future. Picture her in your mind. She is broken, afraid, and vulnerable. At the end of her brokenness, speak to her." So as I try to picture you in my mind, here is what I would say to you. You are beautiful. I don't need to physically see you in order to know that you are indeed beautiful. You were created in the image of Almighty God. Don't you let anyone ever tell you differently. Yes, you might feel broken, because you are. *We all are.* But remember, we are not all broken in the same way. That is okay! Embrace the beauty of the

Paul, a former persecutor of the Christian faith, became the greatest apostle after His encounter with Jesus on the road to Damascus, an encounter that changed his life forever. Paul goes from persecuting Christians to pouring His life into them. As we read through the New Testament, we often find Paul sharing the wisdom God imparted to him. He became a spiritual father to many of his time. And he often made reference to Timothy as His son in the faith, his spiritual son.

Then we have Barnabas. Barnabas lived up to his reputation of being an encourager, the exact encourager Paul needed. People feared trusting Paul because of his previous persecution. However, Barnabas came and walked alongside Paul. He brought him in to the disciples' inner circle, and in not so many words, he said that he was one of them. Barnabas and Paul were peers journeying through life and the advancement of the gospel together. Barnabas was a crucial link between Paul and the fulfillment of Paul's ministry and calling to "go and make disciples."

And now on to Timothy who was referred to as Paul's spiritual son for good reason. Paul made a tremendous investment in Timothy, his faith, and his calling to "go and make disciples." Yes, Timothy was young, but God used him in a mighty way! Paul took Timothy under his wing and poured all that He could into him. But it is clear that Timothy is not the only one being blessed by Paul. Timothy pours into others what Paul pours into him. Many are blessed by Timothy, and the kingdom of God moved forward.

Again, I highly encourage you to take a closer look into their lives. For now, I am going to take a little bit of liberty in order to make this concept of friendship more relatable to us as women. It is what I have used to seek out my own life-giving friendships that I have shared with you throughout this book.

Everyone needs three key people in their lives. First, you need a Pauline (a Paul, also known as a wiser-than-me friend). Next, you need a Betty (a Barnabas, also known as an encouraging peer). And finally, you need a Tiffany (a Timothy, also known as a mentee). And we all need to be each one of these key people to others as well. This is the basis of all life-giving relationships. So I thought I would encourage you by sharing a glimpse into some of those relationships and how they came to be. I'll start with a Tiffany.

I sent a survey needed for the book to a group of women who all fit the descriptions above. One of the questions in the survey was asking for a time that they had seen me choose peace when I could have done otherwise. A "Tiffany" friend responded about a time when she found herself in the midst of an ugly friendship breakup. She had been deeply hurt and was very angry. I could understand her frustration and had heard her out a few times before without asking many questions. (I think it's important to hear each other out before asking questions, too.)

Tiffany's answer to the survey was this: "The day you asked me the difficult questions about the breakup of that friendship, you had tears in your eyes and said 'I know that my next question could cost our friendship, but I have to ask it because it's what God has told me to do. I have heard your side and see the hurt. For that I am sorry. But I now have a question for you. What was *your* contribution to the breakup of the friendship, and what do you need to do about it?' Gina, your peace may not have looked conventional because you were crying and you knew it could cost our friendship, but you had peace knowing you were asking the question God wanted you to ask. And it was the question I needed. As a result, my life has never been the same. Since that day, I have asked myself that question in every conflict I have."

Well, needless to say, our friendship remains strong many years later. The truth is, as difficult as it was to walk through that season, our friendship only became stronger. And yes, she also has had the opportunity to ask me some difficult questions when it has been my turn to be on the receiving end. And for that I am thankful.

Now, do you want to know how Tiffany and I met? My man and I were leading a large Young Adults class on Sunday mornings. The first day as the new leaders of this ministry, I immediately noticed this beautiful girl who made immediate eye contact with me to connect... by rolling her eyes at me with a "If you think we are going to be close friends, whatever" attitude. There had been some misunderstanding when the previous leaders had to transition out, and she just didn't want to risk again. I just smiled back at her and whispered to my man, "Oh, boy, this is going to be fun. I think I just found my new best friend." (I hope you pick up on my sarcasm). That wasn't very life-giving of me.

A few months went by when we felt the Lord asking us to open up our home for a mid-week hang out time and Bible study. This is one of our passions and something we have done in every church we have attended. I highly recommend it. These are great spaces to discover God-given friendships. We didn't know who would come, or if anyone would come at all. We just said at the end of class on Sunday that we would have a homemade dinner and dessert available if they wanted to join us. At this point, there still had not been much connection between me and Tiffany. But God had started steering my heart towards praying for her.

Well, it was now 6:30 on the night we were to start. I was finishing up things in the kitchen when my man leans in and whispered, "You are never going to guess who is the first one getting ready to walk in the door." Yep, you guessed it; it was my new, eye-rolling best friend, Tiffany! Now, I could have greeted her with my own set of rolling eyes. I am not proud of my reaction. But you know us women; we can do that kind of thing and sometimes even justify it! But I couldn't. God had already been softening up my heart towards her and love had already been growing in my heart for Tiffany. Not because I thought it would be easy, but because I know I am not always easy to love either. God had shown me something in her that I had not taken the time to see before. She had been hurt before in relationships and even though she longed for that life-giving relationship (or she would not have kept showing up every Sunday morning to class or had been the first one to show up at our home), she was scared to get hurt again. God told her to keep showing up and stop rolling her eyes at me. You see why I say these are God-given relationships? Because it happened in the least expected way with an unexpected person. When we remain open to trust God for the friendships we need, and when we risk again, He is faithful to show us.

Well, to this day, she remains one of my friends for whom I would jump on a plane any day if she needed me. Or when she calls and says, "It's been a hard season, can I come *home* for a few days?" My answer is, "Yes, when do I pick you up?" We have walked many seasons of life together since. We have cried, and we have laughed. We have prayed each other out of our belly flopping pits and been humbled to celebrate God's mercy through the victories. Yes, it sounds lovely because it is. But now, don't forget about how it all started, with a rolling of the eyes and a thick layer of best friend sarcasm.

Now we move onto a "Betty" story. I am so thankful for the way God always sends the perfect friend our way at just the right moment, those moments when the *brokenness that remains* is ever before us, and there is nothing that we can do about the challenges that come with it. Barnabas was sent to Tarsus to look for Paul and to encourage him as they walked their journeys together. Paul needed someone to encourage him along, given his circumstances and his history. So God sent him Barnabas (Acts 11:25–26). Much like God sent Barnabas to Paul in his time of need, God sent me a Betty on a morning that I desperately needed one and didn't even know it.

It was a Sunday morning when the kids had finally gotten over the flu that had been going around. My man was just a little bit over halfway into a deployment, and there had been a strange guy wandering on our street. Having been stalked before, this only added to my restless night. It had been one of those weeks (one of those weeks when something strange happened while my man was deployed) . The toilet had blown up, and the sprinklers were not working. You get the idea. It was a difficult morning as all of my emotions were getting the best of me. So I was determined to make it to church that morning!

Jacob still needed a lot of my attention after recovering from all of his surgeries. The nursery workers were wonderful and tried to handle his extra needs, but it was usually just a matter of time before my number came up on the screen because Jacob needed me.

So yes, there came my number. As I went around the corner to get Jacob, I could see him being held by someone I had not met before. She was a nursery hall supervisor during a different service that just happened to come in and help that morning. As she saw me coming towards her, she smiled and said, "You must be Jacob's mom." I said, "Yes." And I smiled, but it must have been my eyes overwhelmed with emotion that caused her to smile back and say, "Get back to church. Yes, he will probably cry the entire time, but I promise I will hold him. He will be fine. Get back in church." And as difficult as it was to leave my baby crying, I did. I desperately needed to be in church that morning!

When I came to pick up my boys at the end of the service, she reached over and gave me her number. She said we both had two boys the exact same age. She even offered to have us over for coffee and a playdate. All these years later, even though we don't see each other regularly because there are many states between us, we have taken turns encouraging each other through the different seasons of life. We cheer each other on to continue journeying through ministry. Yep, you guessed it; we have gone on to "make disciples!"

Last but certainly not least, we need to have a "Pauline" in our lives: the wiser-than-us friends who invest in us like Paul invested in Timothy.

I remember when I first fully understood that concept, and I was eager to find her. The funny thing was that she was *already* in my life.

My very first ministry involvement was with one of the most beautiful groups of middle school girls. They were my first group of Tiffanies. I dove into their lives, and before we knew it, we started a small war of toilet papering their friends' homes, their pastor's home, and their cars. My job allowed me a lot of flexibility, so I randomly showed up to have lunch with them at school, or I surprised them with picking them up for a quick and spontaneous ice cream run after dinner. Man, we had so much fun!

Because the girls were middle schoolers, I obviously needed to connect with their parents before doing any of these super fun adventures with them. As a result, I got to know the moms in the group pretty well. They were all wonderful and encouraging to me. And as they saw me pouring into their sweet girls, they poured into *me* and invested in *me*. I am telling you, they were the best middle school years of *my* entire life!

So here I was looking for a Pauline in my life when I asked God to open my eyes to find her. Little did I know I was already seeing her every week when she picked up her daughter after youth group.

I watched her when she didn't know I was watching. She often opened her home for a mid-week study. As a result, I got to see her interact with her children and her husband during those rushed final moments before a bunch of middle schoolers showed up. The leaders often stayed after the meeting to help with some of the clean up. So during those times, I saw her interact when she was tired, too. She didn't do it perfectly, but she did it gracefully and with humility. Now, here is the thing that I will always remember: it didn't matter what day it was or the reason of my stopping by, her Bible was always open on her kitchen table or the counter in her kitchen...always. From time to time, she would casually pull me aside and ask me what God was teaching me, and she would briefly share what He was teaching her.

This only made me long for a Pauline all the more. I was so hungry to dig deeper into the scriptures and grow. Yes, I was praying for my Pauline when she had been standing right in front of me for some time now. It wasn't until I started asking God to keep my motives in check and open my eyes to see her that He said, "There she is! Ask her!"

Ah! Wait! What? I have to ask her? Yes, I did have to ask her. I waited a couple of days longer, and one day after youth group, I just said, "Hi *Pauline, I* was wondering if you would pray about and consider discipling me. I want to dig deeper into the scriptures and learn. I will give you a fair warning; I have a lot of questions!" She smiled and said, "I have been praying for you already. Let me pray specifically about this and talk with my husband about it. I will get back to you soon."

We met weekly for a couple of years. I watched the words in the Bible come alive as she applied scripture to her own life. She used her life experience to teach me when she got it right. She also made it a point to share with me when she stumbled, even though I never would have known. She gently pointed out things she saw in my life and asked difficult questions. And yes, we celebrated the victories and danced on the mountain tops when God answered prayers. She was the last one to see me and pray for me before my step dad walked me down the aisle when I married the man of my dreams, the man she had been praying for me to find.

Our family took a cross country road trip a few years ago after my man's retirement from the Marine Corps. We knocked on Pauline's door for a quick "hello" along the way. And guess what? As I walked up to her door and could see her kitchen table, yes, her Bible was still open right there! We laughed and caught up with each other. And as our families sat in the living room while we went to get water from the kitchen, she pulled me gently aside and said, "It is so good to see you, your man, and the kids. I know we don't have much time. What is God teaching you?"

Yes, sweet friend, we all need a Pauline in our lives. We all need a Betty. And we all need a Tiffany. We all need those life-giving friendships in our lives. These friends will help us walk our journey of *peace in the brokenness*. Chances are that the Pauline, Betty, and Tiffany God has for you are *already* in your life. Maybe they don't look like what you thought they would. They didn't for me. Yet, as I look back through my life, there is no denying that every one of my life-giving friendships has been hand-picked by God.

Exercise

Here are a few questions to consider:

Who is your Pauline?

Who is your Betty?

Who is your Tiffany?

Remember, Paul invested heavily in Timothy. Yet Timothy was not the only one who benefited. No, as Paul would pour into Timothy, he poured into the next generation. Neither of them walked their journeys alone. In what area of your walk with God do you want to grow and learn?

Now identify your specific needs. (Avoid mistaking your needs with neediness by keeping your heart in check and at the foot of the cross.)

Ask God to open your eyes to find the life-giving friendships for which you long. He is the only one who can give them to you. Write names of women below who you respect. Pray about each one. If you ask them to be your Pauline and they say "no" or they "can't at this moment," please don't take it personally. It just means that God has someone else in mind for you. I promise, the Holy Spirit will be faithful to show you. Just make sure your motives are in the right place.

Be careful not to concentrate too much on what your Pauline looks like, or what you need to do or have in order to be a Pauline in a Tiffany's life. All your Pauline really needs to be is someone committed first and foremost to God's Word who has walked a little farther ahead of you. The same applies to you as a Pauline in a Tiffany's life. Seek first His kingdom, His word, and trust Him for the rest. Neither of you will ever have it all figured out; neither of you will have all the answers. But you both have the manual needed, the Bible, in order to navigate through life and the brokenness that remains.

Yes, life-giving friendships take time to develop. Trust needs to be established first, and loyalty must be proven first and foremost to God's Word. Remember not to romanticize friendships. I am telling you, every life-giving friendship that I've had came about in the most unexpected way, with unexpected people. Each one has gone through refining moments, too. They are worth seeking, and they are worth the effort. These life-giving friendships often become the very hands and feet that Jesus uses in our lives to help us keep walking in His peace through the brokenness that remains.

Bibliography

"Broken Heart Syndrome." Mayo Clinic. Accessed February 18, 2016. http://www.mayoclinic.org/diseases-conditions/broken-heart-syndrome/basics/definition/con-20034635.

ESV: Study Bible: English Standard Version. Wheaton, IL: Crossway Bibles, 2007. www.biblegateway.com.

Holy Bible: New Living Translation. Wheaton, IL: Tyndale House Publishers, 2004. www.biblegateway.com.

Holy Bible: NIV, New International Version. www.biblegateway.com.

The Holy Bible: Updated New American Standard Bible: Containing the Old Testament and the New Testament. Grand Rapids, MI: Zondervan Pub. House, 1999. www.biblegateway.com.

Palmowski, Jan. "Nobel Peace Prize." *The Oxford Dictionary of Twentieth Century World History.* Oxford: Oxford University Press, 1997.

"Turn Your Eyes Upon Jesus." Hillsong. Hillsong Music Australia, 2010, MP3.

Voskamp, Ann. *Unwrapping the Greatest Gift.* Illinois: Tyndale House Publishers, 2014.

A free eBook edition is available with the purchase of this book.

To claim your free eBook edition:
1. Download the Shelfie app.
2. Write your name in upper case in the box.
3. Use the Shelfie app to submit a photo.
4. Download your eBook to any device.

Shelfie

A **free** eBook edition is available
with the purchase of this print book.

CLEARLY PRINT YOUR NAME ABOVE IN UPPER CASE

Instructions to claim your free eBook edition:
1. Download the Shelfie app for Android or iOS
2. Write your name in **UPPER CASE** above
3. Use the Shelfie app to submit a photo
4. Download your eBook to any device

Print & Digital Together Forever.

Snap a photo

Free eBook

Read anywhere

CPSIA information can be obtained
at www.ICGtesting.com
Printed in the USA
BVOW08s2317180117
473906BV00001B/5/P